William Ewart Gladstone

The Bank-Charter Act and the Rate of Interest.

Didicated (Without Permission) to the Right Hon (Edition 2)

William Ewart Gladstone

The Bank-Charter Act and the Rate of Interest.
Didicated (Without Permission) to the Right Hon (Edition 2)

ISBN/EAN: 9783744728416

Printed in Europe, USA, Canada, Australia, Japan

Cover: Foto ©Suzi / pixelio.de

More available books at **www.hansebooks.com**

THE

BANK-CHARTER ACT

AND THE

RATE OF INTEREST.

DEDICATED (WITHOUT PERMISSION) TO THE RIGHT HON.

WILLIAM EWART GLADSTONE.

RES POTIUS QUAM AUCTOR.

Second Edition, Enlarged.

LONDON:

SIMPKIN, MARSHALL & CO., STATIONERS' HALL COURT.

1873.

TO THE RIGHT HON.

WILLIAM EWART GLADSTONE,

&c., &c., &c.

Right Hon. Sir,

In the midst of the numerous and more weighty advisers with whom you will doubtless already have conferred, upon the grave and constantly recurring problem which I have feebly, doubtless, endeavoured in the following pages to discuss: I have thus presumed (without permission) to dedicate to yourself my few practical suggestions.

I have ventured to do so, because, in so far as any reform of our Monetary System may be a desideratum, there is, of course, no other than yourself possessing so pre-eminently the strong philanthropic sentiment, and the equally essential qualities of mind, position, and power, which alone could carry such a reform,—even if it were *admitted* to be the great want of the age,—to any successful or practical issue.

For, indeed, it must not be supposed, that any needful reform in this department of Political Economy will escape the hostility of a powerful Plutocracy,—more concerned to uphold the existing state of things, than any Landowner was, in former times, to resist the repeal of the Corn Laws, or any West Indian Proprietor, the fall of Negro Slavery.

I have the honor to remain,

Right Hon. Sir,

Your very humble Servant,

THE AUTHOR.

November, 1872.

PREFACE.

IN presenting to the Public this Second Edition, it may be necessary for the Author to explain that the major portion of the following Treatise was written in the month of November last, during the period when the Rate of Interest, at the Bank of England, stood at *Seven* per cent.; when, also, it was very generally apprehended that the rate would be still further advanced; and when, indeed, some of the leading Metropolitan Press even went so far as strenuously to urge upon the Bank the necessity for adopting that policy to any indefinite extent.

CONTENTS.

ERRATA.

Page 12, Line 23, for *savans, read savants.*

   „ 44, Foot-note, for 15th, *read* 16th.

   „ 74, Line 12, for £100, *read* £60.

   „ 74, Line 13, for £60, *read* £100.

CONTENTS.

BANK CHARTER ACT

AND

THE RATE OF INTEREST.

Any Government would doubtless acquire immortal The Problem. distinction, who should effect a reduction in the annual taxation of the country, to the extent of £20,000,000 sterling.

Such an incentive to a worthy ambition would, at the moment, seem to tempt the present Government to an effort in that direction, in so far as an exorbitant rate of interest may be regarded as one of the heaviest forms of taxation.

To ascertain how far it is, indeed, such a tax, let us take, from the London Clearing House Returns, the amount of commercial bills retired there weekly, at the low figure of £100,000,000 sterling; and, multiplying this sum by the number of weeks in the year, assume that the annual amount, in round numbers, is £5,000,000,000 sterling! Now, at 4 per cent. interest (the difference between the normal rate and **7 per cent.**), what is the result? Not £20,000,000 **merely, but £200,000,000** sterling per annum!

This sum of £200,000,000, then, represents the nature of the recently inflicted tax, which, as we hope to shew, it is in the power of the Government, and of the Government alone, to mitigate, if not to abolish.

It is true that an analysis of this prodigious result might suggest some considerable modifications, but it would still present nothing to affect vitally our argument; while, on the other hand, were we simply to add to the Clearing House Returns the immense aggregate amount of other bills retired annually throughout the provinces, as well as in London itself, but not passing through the London Clearing House, with the aggregate of *cash* payments throughout the country, subject to discount, it would be necessary to add very largely to the colossal sum, which we have deduced for illustration, as being no less than £5,000,000,000 sterling per annum !*

For a moment, then, compare this practical result of an advance of the rate of interest to 7 per cent., with any other possible amount of taxation—with the cost even of our last twenty years' war with France, or with the aggregate annual value of our whole Foreign Trade—and the gravity of the question, now forcing itself into notice, as to the working of the Bank Act of 1844, at once becomes apparent.

How insignificant the financial transactions of the Bank of England, or the value of the entire paper currency, appear in juxta-position with this

* *Vide* Appendix.

gigantic volume of bills of exchange, by means of which the industry and commerce of the country are chiefly carried on and represented.

We have seen the taxative extent of a 7 per cent. rate on this huge mass of floating capital ; but what must be the effect of arresting the course of this vital current of circulation, by the discredit thrown upon it through the Bank of England's inability, when her reserve has been exhausted, to discount even first-class paper? For, in every money-panic since 1844, this frightful result, after the infliction of a 10 and 12 per cent. rate of interest, has ever been the climax of the financial crisis.

Is it matter of surprise, then, that, reverting to former distressing experiences, an incipient alarm should already have seized the country? To all who are familiar with the concomitant events of the past, or even with the recent experience of 1866, it must be palpably evident, that, for a drain of gold, no remedy has yet been, or is now being tried, but that of simply harassing the country with this overwhelming tax of dear money; and yet, so far, without, in any instance since 1844, having succeeded in arresting any special drain of gold, until the Bank of England, through its own exhaustion, and after menacing the country with a state of general bankruptcy, has been obliged to receive aid from the Government, by means of the prompt relaxation of the restrictions imposed upon our money system by the Act of 1844.

The policy of advancing the rate of interest

This oppresive tax of 200 millions per annum, is, however, the great national boon which some of the leading metropolitan press have of late been employing their great abilities to procure for their country. One writer, indeed, who seems in a manner to speak, *ex cathedrá*, upon this and cognate departments of political economy, appeared greatly concerned, first of all, that the incipient infliction of 100 millions of this tax was not sooner imposed; next he deplored that the second 100 millions was not more rapidly superadded; and finally he gave vent to a lament, in effect, that the infliction had not been still further augmented to three, four, or possibly five hundred millions per annum!

From the great urgency with which these writers pressed for the application of their vaunted remedy, an ordinary reader would naturally conclude that the *rule* itself rested on the most certain grounds of experience, and had been settled definitively and past all disputation, like the law of gravitation. And, without doubt, those who assumed the responsibility of prescribing the application of so tremendous a remedy, were bound, at least before doing so, to have ascertained that the rule itself was indeed of such grave authority.

Instead, however, of this being so, we may here say, without the slightest fear of contradiction, that not one of these accomplished writers, nor any other authority, is able to point to even a *single* successful application of their rule, namely,—that to arrest a drain of gold, it is only necessary to advance the rate of interest. We repeat that the whole range of the literature devoted to this question does not supply the experiment of a single test by which to determine the supposed truth of this authoritative canon.

A trivial drain of two or three millions, which must soon be exhausted, and stop of itself, whether the rule were applied or not, would not, of course, furnish an adequate test; while a drain which extended to *ten, fifteen*, or *twenty* millions of gold, would supply both a fair and a decisive experiment.

Now, it will be remembered that, prior to the passage of the Act of 1844, complaints had been constantly reiterated, by Sir Robert Peel and others, that at such times as the foreign exchanges had become adverse to this country, the Bank had ever failed to raise the rate of interest *early enough* to stop the coincident drain of gold.

The combined financial wisdom of the day was therefore engaged to invent some effective remedy for this state of things,—something that should *compel* the Bank to perform more promptly for the public this pre-eminent service! The Act of 1844 was the result; and we freely admit, that, like those formidable instruments of human torture which accompanied the Spanish Armada in its unfortunate invasion of England, the machinery of the Act was most admirably adapted to accomplish its design : for it did most effectually secure, as its result, that, with every million of gold drained from the Bank, another million of the circulating medium should be withdrawn from the Reserve, or from the provinces : thus rendering inevitable the abstraction from a writhing country of the very life blood of its industry and commerce !

Well, then, here was the engine which was to compel an advance in the rate of interest, and so to arrest any future drain whatever, with which the Bank might thereafter be assailed.

The first *application* of this perfected machinery occurred in the eventful year 1847. A serious drain of gold then set in ; the rate was raised. Still the drain went on,—the rate was again raised ; the drain still continued,—the rate was further raised ; the drain seemed, indeed, only to mock at such impotent attempts to arrest it. The rate, however, continued to be advanced, until money commanded 10 and 12 per cent. ; but still the drain was unchecked ! The consequence was that this drain completely exhausted the Bank's Ways and Means, and the *Bank* succumbed !

Here, then, we have an Act well contrived to secure the required advance of interest, and in which it perfectly succeeded ; but, instead of demolishing the drain, the drain completely demolished the Act ; which was therefore suspended.

This was the first fair application of the rule which has been recently upheld by the London press. And the test, we think, was a decisive one.

In two instances since, namely, in **1857** and **1866**, this rule was again enforced; when again, in both instances, the drain signally triumphed over the Act, and the Act had twice again to be rescinded; this grand panacea only sharing the fate of the self-confident hero, who went up to London to set the Thames on fire, and found simply that the Thames extinguished himself.

We have heard of a vulgar kitchen adage that " Cold pudding is the best cure for Love complaints." This is, probably, an old, traditionary, and for anything we know to the contrary, may be a proper remedy for the disease ; but, ridiculous as the thing is, we must here state, that the financial rule we have undertaken to denounce, has no other authority whatever than such as might be produced for this vulgar canon.

This *financial* rule obtains in our day, without the shadow of a pretext to justify it, having been merely passed traditionally down to us, from authority to authority, without once having been brought to any confirmatory experimental test.

The authorities in question seem to have been content to discuss the problem as being only a mere *abstraction*, rather than, as it is, the most vital of all the social and economical questions of the age : in in which every man, woman, and child of the community has the deepest personal interest.

It is no libel on human nature, and, if it were, it is still the fact, that the most educated minds, in the walks both of science and theology, have ever been the readiest to adopt either a fallacy or a heresy; and, in this respect, distinguished names enjoy no superiority over the vulgar multitude.

Who, but the illustrious Stagyrite, could have held in chains, for so many centuries, the entire intellectual world?

Who but a Darwin could have conceived the idea, that the most wonderful intelligence with which, in this world, we are acquainted, was produced from a *mollusc*, or a *monkey*?

Who but a Strauss, could have conceived the idea, that the infinite wisdom and skill displayed in the machinery of the Universe, had no adequate Infinite first cause?

Who but a mental prodigy, like Newman, could have ignominously gone over to the defence of such vagaries as Papal Infallibility, and the fables called Popish miracles?

It is only by analogies of this kind that we pretend to account for the long and pertinacious reign of financial fictions. They have been endorsed by a few eminent *savans,* and have been adopted on such authority without examination.

The money panic of 1847, which originated in the food crisis caused by the failure of the Irish potato crop, was met by the Bank of England in the the following manner: Parliament having assembled early in that year, in order the sooner to devise means for the more prompt importations of food from abroad, the scarcity having advanced the price of wheat at home in that memorable year to 120s. the quarter— the Bank of England was induced to adopt a policy which was directly antagonistic to the humane project of the Government, and to the welfare of the community: for shipments of breadstuffs of anomalous extent being made from the United States, a large balance of exchange was soon established against this country, which could only be paid in *gold*; and a proportionate fall in the premium of exchange on England being the necessary effect, the purchase of bills, at so much below par as 102, left a profit of over 6 *per cent.* on the gold sent from this country to be invested in them; and each operation, with this 6 per cent. profit upon it, could be repeated by steamers within a single month; thus leaving a profit, which was at the rate of 6 per cent. per month, or 72 per cent. per annum, to tempt capitalists into these transactions.

Now, this attractive rate of profit resulted purely from such large importations of breadstuffs, which the anxiety of the Government and the exigencies of the country demanded in so severe a crisis. But the necessary consequence of so procuring supplies of food for our population was, that, at each successive stage of the process, gold was drained away to pay for it from the vaults of the Bank; and therefore, to stop the process, although so sanctioned by Parliament, so far as in her power to do so, the Bank naturally resorted to her own specific, namely, that of raising the rate of interest, with the single object of arresting the efflux of gold; although, under the circumstances, gold was necessarily the only medium of exchange with which the needful supply of food from abroad could be purchased!

The Bank, without doubt, adopted this policy, so inimical to the best interests of the country, as a matter of self interest so far as the Bank herself was concerned; and in the belief which she only shares, it is true, with many of her advocates, that the only expedient necessary to arrest a drain of gold is that of raising the rate of interest, and thereby to transform into a *loss* the profit otherwise accruing from its export.

Now, it is obviously true that if that profit on the export of gold had been only at the rate, say, of a half per cent. or one per cent. per annum, this raising the rate of discount, upon the Bills which formed the basis of each operation, by 2 per cent. per annum, would create the necessary loss contemplated by the Bank, and might possibly arrest an operation which had caused the drain.

But could anything be more futile or puerile, as a policy of self preservation, than for the Bank to hope, by merely raising the rate of interest to any possible point whatever, to stop a drain of gold, which, as this one was, was stimulated by a certainty, which nothing visible could defeat, of a profit of 72 per cent. per annum? Certainly not: for, in the case before us, the buyer of the Bills in America, having an over supplied market at his mercy, had need only to deduct, from the price he would afterwards pay for a Bill, any additional charge upon the transaction which the adverse action of the Bank imposed upon it. It obviously was not possible that merely raising the rate of interest could stop a drain of such character and magnitude, the motive for which was a profit of 72 per cent. per annum!

It is true, however, that this drain was indeed most effectually stopped, in the sequel of affairs, although the profit on the operation must otherwise have remained undiminished : But the stoppage resulted from a state of things which none would wish to see repeated—a general *discredit* throughout the country, the consequence of the complete exhaustion of the Bank's reserve, and of the universal dismay and anxiety, which portended nothing short of general bankruptcy—with the return to a state of barter, through the absolute want of a medium of payment; a state of commercial prostration to which nothing did or indeed could afford relief but the suspension of the Bank Act: to which suspension Sir Robert Peel himself was a consenting party, and that within only three short years after its enactment as being, in his estimation at the time, the only panacea against a frightful money panic, like that which he himself lived to witness under its operation!

Now, we must here beg respectfully to challenge the advocates of the policy of raising the rate of interest in the case just referred to, to show *how* such a policy could, by any possibility, have realised its object under the actual or any analagous circumstances?

If the balance of exchange was really against the country, it strikes us that the only honest policy was, to *pay* it in gold, then the only possible medium of payment; and that any attempt, in such circumstances, on the part of the Bank to oppose obstacles to the payment, was alike unworthy of the Bank and of the commercial honour of the community: there cannot, we think, remain a doubt on this point.

But, apart from considerations of honesty, the policy was simply futile and absurd,—of attempting, by means of any rate of interest whatever, to arrest transactions which grew fairly out of an enormous rate of profit inviting them, and fairly created by such an unavoidable course of events; profit, too, which no rate of interest could by possibility destroy or even touch: and we may fairly challenge the advocates of the policy, in any such an instance of a drain of gold, to show the contrary.

Again, as respects this policy of raising the rate of interest, as a catholicon to be uniformly applied in every instance of a drain of gold, and whatever may be its origin: The recent moderate efflux of gold has not been at all, like that just specified, the consequence of an adverse foreign exchange at any point. Had it been so, we repeat that the only *honest* policy of the Bank would be to abstain from such interference, and permit a just debt of the country to be *paid* in the only medium possible, and that without regard to consequences to herself or to others.

But if, as is generally surmised, the recent drain of our gold is the result merely of Prussia's desire to satisfy, at our expense and inconvenience, a policy of her own; which she is carrying into effect by drawing bills against England, and, after discounting them in London, taking away with the proceeds the gold from the Bank : Here, again, we may fearlessly express the opinion, that the advanced rate of discount in this country can present no effective obstacle which could possibly deter the Prussian Government from so carrying out a national project, for adopting a gold standard in Germany.

There is, however, another method by which, even in such emergency, the Bank of England, if so disposed, might, we think, quite as readily as the Bank of Prussia, adopt similar tactics :—By arranging, say, with the Rothschilds, or otherwise, a credit against which to draw bills on *Prussia;* and, after discounting them there, to bring back gold to this country as fast as Prussia could, by the means at her command, drain it away; and this policy should effectually checkmate, were it to be deemed necessary to do so, the financially hostile move of Prussia; and at the same time avert from ourselves the terrible infliction of an oppressive rate of interest, and also the present alarm, as to what may yet follow of the same disastrous character. *Why,* then, should the Bank of England, it may be asked, attempt nothing at all effective in this matter ? To which, there is but one answer to be given, namely,

B

that it suits the Bank's own interests better to gain
the higher rate of *profits* on her paper issue, by
means of the *higher* rate of interest than she could
by a lower one; and, therefore, to let her store of
bullion fall to the minimum point for that purpose;
knowing, from past experience, that when her reserve has been completely exhausted, the Government must again grant her the usual warrant to
issue paper, irrespective of gold; by which process,
whatever the country may lose in passing through
the ordeal, the Bank truly cannot but gain a golden
harvest of revenue, which to her would not be possible under any other circumstances.

We remember a statement, seriously made by
Lord Overstone, before the Committee of 1840,—to
the effect, that he had, on one occasion, known a
drain of gold to have been arrested by merely
raising the rate of interest to 5 per cent.! In like
manner, we do not doubt, that, should the Bank's
store of gold henceforth increase, and a possible
money crisis be happily no longer apprehended;
the advocates of the recent advance of the rate to 7
per cent. will triumphantly appeal to the increasing
stock of bullion as its simple result. That the two
circumstances will necessarily, in that event, have
been coincident, cannot be denied: but so also were
some other circumstances: for instance, the Mansion
House has all the while continued to overlook the
Bank premises. Unless the relation of cause and
effect can be-*shewn*, and not merely assumed; why

should the Bank not appeal to the latter circumstance for proof, as well as to the former? Is it not a fact, substantiated by her own published returns, that a steady increase of bullion had taken place also while the rate of discount had remained below *three* per cent.? Had there been no advance at all in the rate recently, how can the Bank say that there would not have occurred the same, if not a more rapid, increase of her bullion?

Glad, indeed, should we be, if the Bank authorities, seeing how deeply the public are concerned in the issue, would make the *circumstances* of the subsequent influx a *test* of an abstract philosophy; by merely *investigating* into the *immediate causes* which had induced the particular depositors of it to bring this increase to the Bank; and, also, as to the immediate causes which had induced the foreign correspondents of the depositors to make such remittances to them in gold, instead of doing so in sterling bills; and, if the investigation should bring conviction to the Bank, as we believe it would, that its advance of the rate had nothing whatever to do with those special gold importations,—we trust she may, on future occasions, abstain from inflicting unnecessarily upon the country, not only an enormous tax, but no small amount also of commercial anxiety: But let her, at least, abstain at a time when her stock of bullion is so large as 20 millions!

Now, if raising the rate be an efficacious policy,

when ought this efficacy to show itself? Should it not avert, *before* it is too late, the threatened exhaustion of gold? Or, is it reasonable to say it is efficacious, if, after struggling in vain against the drain by raising the rate to the very highest point, the Bank then ignominously yields, to be saved only by other and more decisive remedies,—a suspension of the Bank Act itself, to avert from the Bank and from the country one common and universal disaster?

If the drain be only a trivial one, it must of necessity soon be exhausted, and so stop of itself: why then raise the rate in such a case as this? If the drain be a *serious* one, like those of 1847, 1857, and 1866, and if the policy then proved so utterly useless for stopping the drain: why resort to it again in such more formidable cases?

We may, indeed, submit to any unprejudiced mind, whether the advocates of this policy of raising the rate to arrest a drain, even were it just and right to attempt it, can possibly escape from the conviction of either the most culpable ignorance on the whole subject, or of the most criminal oppression of the public, by doing mischief on a scale of hundreds of millions sterling, out of mere wanton officiousness? Is it not, indeed, high time that the Bank should be prohibited, in future, from raising the rate on any such frivolous pretext as that of arresting a drain of gold, so completely out of her power; and ought she not now to be *compelled by law* to resort to other more sensible and practicable expedients for maintaining the gold basis of her paper issues?

Since the new sources of supply were opened in California and Australia, in 1848, our imports of bullion have averaged over 20 millions per annum, whether the rate of interest were high or low; and we know of nothing but a money crisis in England, which, by throwing out of gear our commercial relations with the world, could either arrest or delay it; except, indeed, the cause were a large adverse balance of exchange; that is, a *debt* which we must *pay* in gold only, and which, of course, it would neither be just nor possible for the Bank to obstruct by any such policy as that we are now deprecating.

We sometimes meet with observers who are disposed to look with complacency on this policy of the Bank,—which, however, only so much augments her own profits,—as if it were simply adopted in the capacity of a sage monitor of commercial caution; suggesting to all, the prudence of keeping their capital at their bankers, and of abstaining from their ordinary purchases. True; but is there to be no sympathy for the vast body of manufacturers and merchants throughout the community, who, at the time, are necessarily overtaken with their usual stocks on hand? Suppose this suspense of trade, this abstinence from buying, to be protracted indefinitely, through each advance of interest; what must be the wide-spread commercial distress and ruin, what the closing of unremunerative manufactories, and what the misery thereby inflicted on their hapless, though innocent, work-people, who are thus thrown upon parochial relief! To us, it seems that this arbitrary interference with the normal and natural course of markets is, on the part of its agents, simple *barbarity;* while, to the sufferers, it is perhaps the direst national calamity that can be visited upon them.

A main defect in the Act.

When introducing, as the *Complement* of our financial system, the present Bank Charter Act,[*] the late Sir Robert Peel, in reply to his own question, What is a pound? professedly demonstrated that a pound note meant, and could mean nothing else than a specific weight of *gold* into which it was *convertible;* and then proceeded to say:—" I propose, therefore, in the first place, that the Bank, on the basis of a *public debt* of 14 millions, shall issue notes to that amount!" Now, could anything be more illogical than such a sequence to such a proposition? To us, this unpractical conclusion seems just as characteristic of the system based upon it, as the appointment of a Bullion Committee was in 1811, to enquire *why* bullion and the Bank Note then varied in relative value, when the Bank Restriction Act actually restrained the Bank from payment of its notes at all in gold? " I declare," says this eminent authority, " that a Bank note can mean nothing but a definite quantity of *gold: Therefore,* I propose that 14 millions of such notes be issued by the Bank,

* *Vide* Hansard, May 6th, 1844.

without any provision of gold whatever to represent them!" Such is the singular solecism of an accomplished statesman on the most vital of public questions.

There is only one possible assumption on which such 14 millions of notes may be said to be convertible into gold; and that is,—not that the Bank, with only 10s. or 12s. in the £, could ever pay 20s,—but that the public should *never demand payment.* Such also is the assumption relied upon by Sir Robert Peel; and, for that reason, the Act of 1844 was designed to work in the following manner: Some special drain of gold, as in 1847, might take out of circulation, or from the reserve in the Banking Department, an amount of Bank notes, and these being presented for gold at the Issue Department, such notes were extinguished, and thus, to that extent, *the circulation became contracted.* The ordinary circulating medium was next again to be contracted, by the Bank's refusal to discount commercial bills; the same example being also followed by discount banks throughout the country; who, in the existing scarcity of money, would not or dared not part with it, and so locked it up from its usual channels of circulation. This universal scarcity of money, so produced, was to be again augmented by a further expedient of the Bank of England; which was to sell, or hypothecate its securities, so as to gain other additional notes from circulation: by all which processes the vast current of some 5,000 millions sterling of commercial Bills was to be obstructed or arrested; the acceptors of them driven hither and thither throughout the land, like Pharaoh's bondmen in quest of what had ceased to exist—the means of providing for the payment of their acceptances ; while the holders of such bills were trembling under the discredit thus thrown upon their paper; sales of produce and manufactures, at same time and from the same causes, became alike impracticable; great industrial works were contracted or closed, the workers being cast adrift; until, indeed, an impending National Bankruptcy,—together, no doubt, with the Bank's inability, through the exhaustion of her Reserve, to pay even the cheques of the Government—had, by such imperative motives, compelled the sanction of the suspension of the Act of 1844, which had, as in 1847, produced this confusion !

Now, for what purpose was all this terrible mischief set in motion? To use a familiar proverb —it was in order simply to make " an empty sack to stand upright." It was designed to make Bank notes *scarce*, by an expedient which forms the most conspicuous feature of the system : namely, by their arbitrary " *contraction*"; and so to stave off, through this artificial scarcity, any public demand for payment of that portion of the Bank's paper which had not a particle of *gold*—indeed, nothing whatever in the Bank but a public debt—to represent it !

A commercial house, if brought into similar circumstances, would, of course, call the *whole* of its creditors together, and divide fairly amongst them its assets, *pro rata* with its liabilities to each : but, here, it is only for all *first*-comers to get *twenty*-shillings in the pound, and,—" De'il tak' the hindmost."

What then is another main defect of the Act of 1844? We answer: The Act is entirely the product of a mind possessed of only *one idea* on the subject, and that idea is *convertibility*. But, relying on this expedient of *contraction*,—which only throws the system upon the other horn of the dilemma, and, we have seen, is synonymous simply with public confusion,—the Act destroys *itself* : as, indeed, every measure must which is invented like this one, to be an instrument merely of public torture. Within twenty years, this notable Act, when its operation had become publicly intolerable, was *three times* suspended! On an apposite occasion, the authoritative Biblical canon was once propounded : " The Sabbath was made for man, and not man for the Sabbath." But *here* the *public* are made for a system ; which, instead of being only the handmaid and fosterer of the national prosperity, is constituted its most tyrannical oppressor! Sir Robert Peel was intent to secure simple convertibility ; forgetful that, in a civilised country, the state of Barter is an impossibility ; and that, even if convertibility itself should fail, we must still have a *circulating medium;* although it should only

(margin note: A second grave defect in the Act.)

be—like that which has lately worked such marvellous effects in America—the *next* best in quality. Sir Robert Peel's policy fatally resembles that of the luckless mariner, who avoided Scylla only to be ship-wrecked on Charybdis: for, while he assumes, *suo more*, that convertibility had been secured by the Act of 1844—why, as a great public exigency, has its operation been suspended on three occasions; and, on the first—*with his own consent and approval!*

If the theory be a true one, that a high rate of interest will arrest the efflux of bullion, and, *vice versa*, that a low rate will promote it,—how is it to be accounted for, that gold is incessantly flowing into our ports, though our rate of interest be only 2 per cent.; while it is 6 per cent. and upwards in those countries from whence we receive such gold, —America and Australia, for example?

When, however, the course of Exchange is *adverse* to a country, gold will leave it inevitably, irrespectively of any possible rate of interest. The adverse balance is shown by the *excess of bills* offered upon the country in foreign markets; and which excess the ordinary demand for such bills, for purposes of remittance, is insufficient to take off the market; the rate of Exchange will fall to such a point, below par, as will create another class of bill-buyers, namely, those who operate for the sake of the *profit* on importing gold.

Now, in such a situation of Exchanges, the

buyers of bills, having the market entirely at their
mercy, through an excessive supply of bills for sale,
can obviously dictate their own terms of purchase ;
and if they find the *cost* of the operation augmented
by an enhanced rate of discount charged upon such
bills, they can still maintain their rate of profit, by
merely refusing to buy such bills, except at a *further*
reduced rate of premium, which it is obviously
within their power to exact.

How, then, can merely raising the rate of discount obstruct this traffic, until the balance between
the two countries has thus been paid in gold, and
the exchange between them so restored to par ?
Whatever obstructed such payment of the balance,
must only maintain a lower rate for bills below par :
which difference solely creates the profit on such exports of gold, and stimulates them.

Again : If such bills were purchased at so little
below par, as to leave a net profit on importing
gold, of only* half per cent., and the gold could be
transported hence to a continental city in less than
a week, (or rather, we should say, two or three times
a week), the operation would still yield a profit at
the rate of 20 per cent. per annum ; but if the rate
of profit, (as in America in 1847), were over 5 per
cent. per *fortnight*,—and by means of the cable, an
operation could now be completed within a fortnight,—the profit would thus be at the rate of 120
per cent. per annum : what effect, therefore, could
our raising the rate of discount, to any possible

point, have in stopping a drain under such circumstances? Obviously, none at all.

It appears to us high time indeed, that the Bank should resort to other expedients to replenish her sinking reserve : and, although at some little cost to herself, she should regard such cost as the needful premium of insurance, so to speak, against a recurrence of such exhaustion as she exhibited in 1847, 1857, and 1866 ; and, during her periods of affluence, that she should possess herself of an adequate amount of securities, such as she could convert into gold abroad at the time of any future drain, and so maintain her needful reserve, without inflicting an oppressive rate of interest on the public ; and without reducing herself to such discreditable straits, (such, indeed, as would ruin any other mercantile concern) as to render herself unable to provide the necessary ways and means to meet the demands upon her, without such aid from the Government, as the Government could only afford by breaking through an Act of Parliament, devised by the wisdom of Sir Robert Peel to meet this very exigency !

Thoroughly convinced as we are, that Sir Robert Peel's financial measure was framed in utter misconception both of what its actual effects upon the Bank herself would be, and of the monetary exigencies of the country ; yet we venture to assert, that neither the singular humiliation of the Bank, nor the unparalleled sufferings which the community have experienced under it, would need to have become matter of history, had that measure been merely sustained by a *penalty* of the following kind:—That, should the Bank fail to keep up, through all periods, a reserve of bullion, sufficient to prevent any advance of interest beyond 3 per cent., her Charter should be forfeited,—the Act of 1844 would have been maintained in its integrity, and a money panic, such as we have since witnessed, would have been rendered impossible.

That it was in the Bank's power to have maintained the required reserve, we need only appeal, for proof, to what the Bank actually *accomplished* under such legislative mandate, when, after our French war, with only inconvertible paper too, she was able to bring home from abroad 30 millions of gold! *

The United States' Government, at the present day, has as great an interest at stake as the Bank of England has, in maintaining a certain stock of bullion. The American Government has engaged to pay, in gold, the interest upon her debt; and any failure to do so must involve the national credit. But America enforces the needful provision of gold for the purpose, by requiring the Duties on commodities to be paid to her in *gold*. This is an obvious and practical method of providing gold. But were that Government to rely, as the Bank of England does,

* " By reverting to specie payments, we (that is the Bank) made an unexpected purchase of *thirty millions* of gold. The gold imported into Great Britain, to enable the Bank to resume specie payments, was not taken from any particular country or district, but was drawn from the market of the world."—*McCulloch's Dict. Art. Bank of England*, p. 75.

on anything so illusory as raising the rate of interest
to produce the needful influx of gold, what could
possibly result, but exhaustion and bankruptcy, as it
does periodically to the Bank ? The relation of the
rate of interest to supplies of gold, is simply the
proverbial one of Tenterden Steeple to Goodwin
Sands !

We do not intend to assert, that there is no
export of gold that might not be lessened by a sudden advance in the rate of discount. The drain,
however, in that event, must be only of the most
trivial character ; one that would as soon exhaust
itself if let alone ; and what we do maintain is, that
such a case is only a rare exception to the opposite
rule. To stop any *serious* drain resulting from an
adverse exchange, is, if it were possible, only to
augment the fall in the premium of bills, and the
profit on exporting gold : but when the adverse
balance has been paid, by the export of gold, the
exchange of itself will return to par, and so stop
legitimately the drain.

Nothing, indeed, is to us more marvellous than
the purpose and attempt to deal with a drain of
gold in this manner. The purpose is, of course,
that a balance of Exchange, it may be 15 or 20
millions sterling, as in 1847, is *not* to be paid,
though *owing ;* but the payment in *gold,* the only
possible medium, is to be absolutely prevented.
Doubtless that is the purpose. Can anything be
more monstrous than this conception ? Can any

act be more *unjust* or *dishonourable?* Yet it is the policy justified and recommended by Lord Overstone and his distinguished school, namely, that of a *debt justly owing* by the country, payment *is to be avoided* if possible. Any system which can only be maintained by such shifts ought surely, by a great nation, to be treated with abhorrence and contempt. The futility of the *attempt* to carry into effect this purpose, of avoiding the payment of a just debt, by raising the rate to stop the drain, has truly been as conspicuous as its injustice!

Foreign Bills, drawn on England, may be *discounted*, of course, either in the place where they are drawn, or in England. The choice will be determined by the holder of the Bills, for his own convenience, and by the comparative rate of discount. But *discounting* a Bill cannot affect the *balance of Exchange* between the two countries; because the Bills referred to, even should they not be discounted at all, would still, of course, have to be paid at *maturity*. And, if it were otherwise, can it be anything but the very climax of absurdity to tax the country to the extent, perhaps, of 100 millions sterling, by raising the rate, with the object simply of preventing the discount of comparatively the most trivial amount of such bills?

The effect on the balance of trade would be precisely the same, in the case of Bills drawn in England on a continental city, and whether discounted or not.

Nor is it to be supposed, that *any* advanced rate

of interest would be allowed, by those requiring the *gold*, to arrest a drain that should be caused either by the Prussian authorities, for the introduction of their new gold standard; or by the authorities of France, for the purpose of obtaining the means of paying the German indemnity.

Now, what, on its own principles, was a further grand defect of the celebrated Act of the late Sir Robert Peel? Mainly this, that, without requiring any adequate *provision* to maintain its bullion basis, the Bank's *emoluments* were, on the contrary, made proportionate to the *decline*, instead of to the increase, of its store of the precious metals; so that, whenever through an efflux of bullion, the Bank should advance its rate to 6 per cent., its net profit, upon the 14 millions of its notes issued on the Public Debt,—which profit Sir Robert Peel showed* was some £100,000 at 3 per cent.,—should rise to some £500,000 at 6 per cent., and to £900,000 when the rate, owing to the drain of bullion being unchecked, rose to 9 per cent! In this manner, the Bank Act necessarily raises up for the Bank an interest which is the most adverse to that of the public; by augmenting its emolument, in the exact ratio of the exit of bullion, and consequent advance of interest.

---

* Vide *Hansard*, 6th May, 1844.—Sir Robert Peel said : "The Bank is to retain the privilege of issuing notes on securities to the amount of £14,000,000. On an interest of 3 per cent., the gross gains of the Bank upon this total issue would be £420,000." "The *net* profit of the Bank, to be derived from the issue of notes, will not probably exceed the sum of £100,000." Each advance of the rate of interest by 3 per cent. would, of course, add to the Bank's profit another £420,000, the *expenses* of the issue being all paid out of the first 3 per cent.

Assuming, therefore, that the inefficacy of the Bank's sole expedient for arresting a drain of bullion, until the trade and industry of the country have been disastrously paralysed,—is placed beyond doubt by the history of every monetary crisis since the passing of Sir Robert Peel's Act,—we venture to suggest that some more hopeful experiment may now be tried—some plan which, while it would afford the country protection from incessant and extreme alternations in the value of money, should also make more certain and visible provision for maintaining permanently such a stock of bullion, as should supersede entirely the disastrous policy of enforcing oppressive rates of interest for such a simple object, —simple indeed when, since 1848, some £400,000,000 of gold alone, from Californian and Australian mines, have been added to European stores of that commodity.

Were the Government to make an experiment of the following kind, they would probably demonstrate how facile an operation would secure a contingent supply of gold to the required amount. Let them take the matter entirely out of the hands of our money dealers, whose natural craving is ever for the highest rates, and invite a *tender* from the house of Rothschilds*,—of a rate of commission, at which

* Suppose the Messrs. Rothschilds, who are next to omnipotent in such matters, to accept this responsibility for a commission of one per cent. per annum, on say five millions,—the difference between the sum of 20 millions and 15 millions of bullion in the Bank,—and that for *twenty years* afterwards the bullion were never to fall below 20 millions; nor the rate of interest, in consequence, to rise above three per cent.: the effect, of course, must be the steady growth of our that House would undertake to maintain permanently for the Bank of England a sum in bullion of *twenty millions*—the Government, of course, issuing an equivalent amount of 3 per cent. Consols, as a basis for the operation. The rate tendered, would doubtless be a very minute fraction of the tax now imposed for the same object. Could any operation be more simple than that we have suggested? Could any conception be more monstrously irrational or ruthless than the process now in operation, of inflicting an imposition at the rate of 200 millions sterling, (which may yet be doubled before the game is played out) and all for no other contemplated result, than merely replenishing the Bank with an additional *three* or *five* millions of *gold:* upon which infinitesimally contracted basis, a supon the apex of an inverted pyramid, our ponderous commercial fabric is thus made to rest—and, by the necessary sympathy involved in our extended foreign·relations, the commercial prosperity of the greater portion of the world!

Our problem, then, is simply,—How a great Empire like our own, may effectively apply the most

national prosperity, for twenty years, uninterrupted by any frightful money panic like those of 1847, 1857, and 1866. This commission, amounting to £50,000 per annum, would therefore be charged to the country. But how many times would it be refunded to the Exchequer, by an increased Revenue, from the greater consumption of Dutiable commodities, which has always distinguished prosperous periods: to say nothing of the thrift and contentment of the population at large, and the greater progress of the nation in all that is vital and valuable to a country. So happy a result would doubless render it profitable for us as a nation to pay even ten times £50,000 for so great a boon! We have for a long period been paying the Bank, as a minimum, £100,000 per annum, and often at the rate of a *million* per annum: And—For what?

infinitesimal fraction of its unlimited resources to the
object of providing permanently for the Bank, an
additional contingent Reserve, of a *few millions*
only, of bullion : so as, by such provision, to save the
most eminent of commercial nations from the stigma
of attempting to evade the due payment of its foreign
debts, by any such disreputable shifts as the enforcing
of a ruinous rate of interest ; and also to avert the
periodical visitation of a calamitous Money Panic.

We venture now to propose (amongst various
other suggested schemes), one which is, at least, a
practicable measure : That, after satisfying all just
claims of the Bank of England upon the Government, the Bank's Power to issue Notes be withdrawn, on the next discussion of its charter in
parliament; and be transferred to a *Government*
department, who should thereafter issue a *National*
convertible currency, to take the place of the current
notes of the Bank of England.

The Bank of England now issues only in exchange for securities of equivalent value. The
proposed National issues would, of course, be made
only on the same footing; but, in the latter case,
the bullion and other valuable securities, received by
the Government Bank in exchange for its issues,
would become the property of the *nation;* and to any
needful extent, would therefore be available for
investment in interest-bearing Funds of good Foreign
Governments, including American. Such foreign
funds to be afterwards turned to profitable account,

as an efficacious preventive of future financial panics:
for these funds, which would yield a good rate of
interest so long as retained, would also serve for
conversion into gold abroad, to replenish our bullion basis under a drain, as fast as any foreign demand could draw it away.

By so simple and facile a process is it indeed
possible to supersede the present ruinous policy
of raising the rate of interest for the same object.

And, as a further effective means of permanently maintaining an adequate stock of bullion—
when the ordinary *influx* of Gold should, at any
future period, be so large as, under the existing
system, would reduce the value of money *below* 3
per cent. by augmenting excessively the Bank's
Reserve—we again propose that, instead of per-
mitting *too low* a rate, this *surplus* of redundant Gold
be also invested in good foreign funds, to be likewise held against the future recurrence of any
special drain of bullion ; when the operation of
reselling such securities for Gold could be repeated.

Thus, on the one hand, by merely investing in
foreign funds our surplus importations of gold ; and,
on the other hand, realising these funds abroad
again for gold to the required extent, the area of
fluctuation in the rate of interest must be circumscribed and limited; and, by judicious management,
the rate might obviously be prevented from greatly
varying at any time from the present normal rate of
about 3 per cent.

By an arrangement with the present *Issue* Department of the Bank of England, that department might
act for and represent the Government therein, and thus
the proposed plan could with very little difficulty be
carried into effect; the Bank of England, at the
same time, could be remunerated, by being allowed
a rate of commission, which should *increase* as the
stock of bullion *augmented*, but be diminished in
the ratio of its decrease; and by this method, the
Bank of England might still, if desirable, be com-
pensated for its services to the same extent as it is
now. Thus, the Government Issue department, by
the exercise of a prudent foresight, would be
enabled not only to avert a recurrence of the present oppressive rates of interest; but also more
effectively to ensure its professed object,—the maintenance of an adequate bullion basis for a *National*
currency of convertible paper: than which nothing
confessedly could possibly be more secure to the
holders.

Such a National Bank note currency would
possess the *National* security, and would therefore
supersede the necessity for a *security* basis, like that
of the present Bank's Dead Weight. Instead of
this Dead Weight, the proposed Bank of Issue,
should purchase, with a portion of its paper, an
adequate amount of good current funds of Foreign
Governments, such as could be promptly resold for
gold when necessity arose. For that purpose, the
present Bank's Dead Weight would be useless;

while good foreign funds, so used, would accomplish the desired end promptly and effectually. This basis then, with that of the Funds, and gold and silver, would serve every necessary purpose; and the National paper would be issued in exchange for such valuable securities to any required extent; provided only that a due proportion of bullion should, by the means suggested, or otherwise, be always maintained.

A national currency, possessing the guarantee of the *State* is, of course, independent of any other basis, as a question of *security* merely. But, with regard to the separate question of its *convertibility* into gold—a quality to be desired as a matter of public convenience, — the provision necessary to secure it would be identical with that required in the case of private Banks of Issue.

Inconvertible Currencies: America.

The current note circulation of the United States of America presents, however, a striking example and demonstration of what a purely *artificial* currency, constituted by a great nation for a patriotic object, may accomplish: since by means of a national and regulated, though *inconvertible* issue of paper money, a five years' civil war, of unexampled proportions, has recently been conducted to a successful issue, at an unparalleled cost of 500 millions sterling, within that short period; equalling that of our own twenty years' war with France: and, what is yet more instructive, the huge debt, so created, is now being rapidly extinguished, by means of the same *inconvertible* paper. And it must be admitted that, for securing either of these grand national objects, a so-called *convertible* currency, through its restrictive inexpansibility, must have proved only an ignominous failure,—acting, as it ever does on the country subject to it, just as a *solid metallic* coat would upon a growing youth ; or as the shoe of a Chinese lady restrains the growing foot!

To substantiate the absolute truth of these comparisons, let it be supposed that a prosperous condition of industry and employment in the country, required the *additional* sum of *ten millions* of specie, for the payment of wages to the additional workers. This required sum would, of course, gradually flow into circulation from the Bank of England, and its bullion reserve would be thereby reduced to 10 millions : now, with interest at 7 per cent. while the reserve is still nearly 20 millions, what must be the situation of the Bank, and the financial condition of the country, if that reserve, although from circumstances so much to be desired, should be so reduced to only 10 millions ?

The effect would necessarily be identical with what occurred in the instances of the crises of 1847, 1857, and 1866 : the progress of the Nation must

---

* To us, it is indeed a melancholy reflection, and one withal worthy of grave pondering, that, whenever the United States shall return again to a convertible currency, the liquidation of this National Debt must cease. Our own Sinking Fund, devised for a similar object, we know, ceased to receive any important payments after the abrogation of the Bank Restriction Act. No currency, doubtless, but one that was able to *sustain* a great war, need be expected to *liquidate its cost.*

again be thrown back for years, until it could again contrive to restrict its expanding prosperity within the limits of this inexorable metallic coat!

The money panic of 1866, if we do not mistake, was caused by just such a simple transfer of specie from the Bank to the *Provinces*, for industrial circulation there during a period of prosperous activity. There was no special foreign drain in that year, the imports greatly exceeding the exports of bullion.

Had the Bank been able to keep up its own reserve, as well as to supply this innocent demand upon it, the revulsion could not then have occurred as it did.

Till lately the country, during the present year and some time previously, had been culminating again towards the same enviable climax of prosperity. The recent action of the Bank, however, has already initiated the usual baneful reaction; and every business man, through the length and breadth of the land, is obliged to consider *what*, and *when* the end will be : looking indeed morning after morning, with the most intense anxiety to the daily movements to or from the Bank, of every £100,000 of gold : so trivial a circumstance as this, as matters now stand, having really more influence upon a great nation's prosperity, than any other event, be it what it may, can possibly exercise upon it.

Surely our financial system must be fatally vitiated by some gross illusion or defect, or how

could such a doleful fact arise, that the condition
of national prosperity, to which all things naturally
tend, should prove the very result which, of necessity, involves the most calamituous of national
reverses! Were the country, by possibility, ever to
be blessed by Providence with such a degree of
prosperity, that the entire number of able-bodied
paupers and unemployed persons in the land, should
find profitable employment, and the wages of the
working classes be further augmented generally
by some 10 per cent. only; the consequence must
inevitably be, under the existing currency system,
a money panic of the most formidable character;
and this simply because the increased amount of
gold and silver requisite for merely paying the
wages of these labouring classes, being taken out
of the Bank, the Bank must collapse through
the simple *transfer* of so much gold, and the national
prosperity with it. Is the preservation of some
five millions of bullion in the Bank, an adequate
compensation to the country for the misery thus
periodically inflicted upon it, by the fatal means
employed to secure that comparatively trivial
benefit? Not so, certainly!

Though ourselves giving every preference to a
convertible national currency, when accompanied, as
doubtless it may be, by adequate and *certain* provision for the prompt replenishment of its specie basis
whenever necessary; yet it is only just to the merits
of a currency wanting in that quality, to recognise

42

the undoubted powers which even *inconvertible* paper may possess for the advancement of the national prosperity.

Besides the now extant example of the United States, we may, for additional evidence of this fact, refer to the unparellcled commercial and industrial advances, as well as the military achievements of our own country, during a twenty years' Bank Restriction Act; in which, if we are not mistaken, there was, at least, an immunity from the calamitous money panics to which we have since been so painfully familiarised; if we except what occurred in 1811, through the natural dismay and discredit produced by the *possibility* that the deliberations of the Bullion Committee, then sitting, might have resulted in an Act of Parliament reinvesting the country in its repressive metallic coat, by the return to so-called convertibility. No doubt, the fear that an early ignominious peace with Napoleon must be the result, led to the postponement of that step. Had it been otherwise, that great European contest, through necessary failure of the sinews of war, could not have been conducted by us to a successful issue; nor could the country have gained a military immortality by its subsequent victories in the Peninsula and at Waterloo.

Indeed, it may well be, with many observers, a matter of regret, that a monetary power of such vigorous efficacy, and which had accomplished for us so much during that protracted war; had not afterwards been allowed to demonstrate also what it was able to effect during the subsequent long reign of peace ; by more fully developing all the national resources in every department of industry. To that view of the case we readily concede the admission, that at least the disastrous money panics, which under the existing money system, have occurred periodically since, must have been an impossibility.

It is, indeed, more than probable, besides, that the National Debt itself, within a comparatively few years, must also have been paid off; judging from the large sums continuously paid into the Sinking Fund, after that fund had been constituted for the purpose; but which large payments have long since almost entirely ceased, under our present restrictive money system.

Another striking demonstration of the re- Inconvertible Currencies : cuperative vigour which even inconvertible paper, France. when issued from a responsible source, can infuse into a prostrated nation, is furnished by the case of France, under the Revolution of 1848. One of the coincidents of that grave political event, had been to drain away the specie of the Bank of France, and so to withdraw the Bank note circulation, to a most distressing extent, from the country at large. The Bank in consequence, and as a matter of absolute necessity, was empowered to issue its notes irrespective of any specie basis. The Bank did so; its printing press being kept at work night and day to supply an extraordinary demand upon it, until the Bank had again furnished

the provinces with a circulating medium; discounting freely at all points, besides appointing agencies
in every commercial port and city, to make liberal
advances to those who applied for them, on produce
and commercial property held in stock. The singular
result of this patriotic care for the interests of commerce, on the part of the Government, was, that
within twelve months, it had restored complete
prosperity at all points to the industrial and commercial interests of France; but, what must be
more striking to believers in the virtues of a *gold*
basis *only*, this inconvertible paper, judiciously
applied, proved the means also, within the same
year, of refilling the Bank coffers with *Gold*, and
introducing, besides, into the country circulation,
specie to the value of some 500 millions of francs!

Curious to say, in an article on this subject,
in the previous year, the *Times* newspaper had
given vent to a lamentation over this issue of inconvertible paper, as being one of the most fatal
incidents of the Revolution!

But early in the following year, another editorial appeared in the same columns, in which the
writer was forced to admit its complete success; at
the same time passing an elaborate panegyric upon
the Count d'Argout's management of the financial
affairs of the Bank and of the country at so critical
a period.*

While on this topic, we may again refer to the

* Vide *Times* of February 16th, 1849.

45

historical fact confirmed by Mr. McCulloch,[*] that
the Bank of England, acting under the imperative
mandate of the Legislature, which, after the war
above referred to had determined on a return to
specie payments,—found no difficulty then, although
having only its own inconvertible paper to work
with, in shortly introducing gold and silver into the
country from abroad, to the extent of some 30
millions sterling! We can only here express the
wish and prayer, that the Bank,—at the present
juncture, when it ought to be more in her power to
do so, and is certainly as much needed,—would
accomplish only a fraction of the same result with
her now *convertible* paper : and, it need not be
doubted, she would promptly do so, were she only
to be impelled by a similar *mandate* of the Legislature. Such a step on her part would at any rate
save the country from the humiliation to which it
was brought in 1839, by our being obliged to
borrow from France some two millions sterling in
gold to replenish the Bank's store; which store, for
three or four years, did not then exceed in all some
three-and-a-half millions! These were the two grave
facts which additionally led to Sir Robert Peel's Act
of 1844, and which Act, so far simply as respects the
mere prevention of the Bank's store falling again
to so very low a point, may be said, so far, to have
proved successful.

Those who are familiar with our financial his- The Bullion Committee of 1811 : Its ob-ject.
tory, will be aware that the Bullion Committee of

* Vide Com. Dict. Art. Bank of England.

1811 was appointed with the special object of inquiring into the causes of the alternations in the price of gold, under the Bank Restriction Act, and while of course the price was no longer *fixed* legislatively. With the report of that committee before us, we must confess ourselves much struck with admiration at the naive simplicity, not to say the manifest ignorance of the matter in hand displayed in the suggestion of such an inquiry; as well as by the questions put to the several witnesses who were examined by the committee. Let us fancy, for a moment, the United States of America, whose currency is just now in precisely the same condition of inconvertibility as ours was in 1811,—now appointing a committee of the Legislature, to inquire *why* the price of gold,—which of necessity now *fluctuates* daily in that country, under the natural law of supply and demand,—does not remain constantly at par with Greenbacks, as it used to do, before the civil war, with paper; or fancy, at this day, the House of Commons appointing a committee to inquire, why the price of gold now remains *stationary*, and does *not* fluctuate daily, under the law of supply and demand, as it did under the Bank Restriction Act?

The mariner at sea, on finding that the ship's compasses did not act, would not, we presume, deem it necessary to inquire into the cause, if he were informed that the maker of the instrument had omitted to supply the magnet to the dial. Nor do we suppose, that the Government, on being informed that a line of battle ship had just been lost from a similar neglect, would deem any inquiry necessary into the cause of the disaster. Nor would such an inquiry be deemed necessary, should one of our costly public edifices suddenly fall down in ruins, if it were generally known that the foundation had been previously undermined! And yet it is historically true, that, in 1811, a committee of the House was appointed, for the purpose of inquiring *how it was*, that *gold* then had *varied* in price, although it was publicly known and understood, that the Bank Restriction Act, then in operation, had several years previously rescinded the arbitrary law which aforetime *fixed* its price at £3 17s. 10½d. the ounce, and had placed that commodity again under the natural law of supply and demand. Yet strange as, indeed, it may be to any one acquainted with the subject, that committee was really appointed for no other object, than to institute so simple an inquiry! Mr. F. Horner's celebrated resolutions were the grand result; and upon those resolutions, to which the late Sir Robert Peel avowed himself a convert, our present money system has been subsequently based. To us, it seems that the very *origin* itself of a system, which has since, by repeated experiments, been found periodically to work such national mischief, could portend no other than the actual result so painfully realised by us.

Were the Bank of England the sole owner of

48

the stocks of *Wheat* in the country, and were she compelled to sell that commodity at no other price than £3 17s. 10½d. per quarter; and to pay such price only for any further quantity, whenever offered to her for sale; the price of *wheat*, too, must be absolutely *fixed* in the same way precisely as that of gold is now fixed by Law.

But how any Legislature, having recently rescinded the Law which alone had so *fixed* the price of a commodity, should afterwards enter upon a solemn inquiry why it was that, what was no longer so fixed, should now naturally *fluctuate* with the supply, like any other commodity so situated, does appear to us a severe reflection upon the capacity of the House to deal with the question; and it so far goes to confirm the truth of a remark made by an eminent member of the House, that our Legislature has ever persistently declined to think and act for itself, in anything relating to this most vital and fundamental question of our times; preferring rather to follow the lead of any prominent member of the House, than bring to bear upon it the exercise of their own unbiassed judgment and common sense.

The foregoing suggestions, of course, have reference to some thorough reform of our Banking system, the discussion of which must precede any future renewal of the Bank of England's charter.

The immediate exigency.

But the more immediate question presented now is—as to what the Government should do,

under an existing 7 per cent. rate of interest, and
in the incipient stage of a money panic; which may
yet grow to frightful dimensions, for any means
adapted to avert it, except the abortive one of a
calamitous further advance in the rate of interest—
abortive, because every application of it, as a
remedy aforetime, has demonstrated it to be so.

On this point,—the utter futility of an advanced
rate of interest, to counteract a special drain of
bullion, we may challenge contradiction, while we
simply appeal to the comparatively recent experience of 1847, 1857, and 1866: on which grave
occasions, relief was afforded, not by dear money,
but by the temporary suspension of the Act of 1844
which had produced it, and the *reduced* value of
money which was the necessary sequence.

No one, we presume, doubts that the same
Government interposition must again be repeated, if
the present menacing situation should mature into
an aggravated monetary crisis, like those which distinguished the memorable years referred to.

If such, then, be the *only* and inevitable final
remedy, why should not the Government, beforehand, *at once* apply it as a *preventive?* The orthodox
method of raising the rate of interest, and arresting
the circulation of some 5,000 millions sterling
of bills, has surely been sufficiently tried already,
and found wanting. If so, can there be any such
danger in experimenting with a specific of an

D

opposite and more grateful tendency—a remedy which, instead of throwing out of gear our whole industrial machinery, supplies the only lubricating oil which can enable it to work uninterruptedly, smoothly, and successfully.

The immediate exigency. With regard then to the immediate exigency, we respectfully submit, that should the Bank proceed to raise its rate to *eight* per cent., the only remedy resorted to on former occasions, be *at once* applied; but, that it be applied only in the identical manner sanctioned by the late Sir Robert Peel himself, in 1847: which was, by means of a Treasury warrant, authorising the Bank of England to issue the required amount of its notes, irrespective of its stock bullion; but at no lower rate, for the moment, than 8 per cent.: the outside rate previously having been 10 to 12 per cent! The effect of Sir Robert Peel's method of relief, under those circumstances, was instantaneous: because practically it was felt to be a reduction of the rate from *twelve* to only *eight* per cent. Contrast that method with the course adopted during the money panic of 1866; when the relaxation of the Act was accompanied by a *menace* on the part of the Government, that the rate of interest might, notwithstanding, be afterwards indefinitely *raised!* The high rate was therefore oppressively continued at even *ten* per cent. for many months; the relief was slight indeed, except to the Bank itself; and the calamitous effects upon the trade and industry of the country, were felt for as many following *years:* And even now, with nearly 20. millions of Gold in the Bank,—a store unprecedented in the late Sir Robert Peel's day, when 15 millions was deemed ample stock enough to keep the rate at *three* per cent.,—we have a rate of *seven* per cent.! Surely some new and fatal counsels have prevailed in the Bank Parlour, since 1847, and during a period, too, when the enormous expansion of our commerce required every possible financial succour, instead of this hostile and ruinous policy.

The issue of such a Treasury Warrant would at once restore public confidence, in an adequate supply of money being maintained; and the rate of interest would gradually fall, under favourable foreign exchanges and the influx of bullion. Such, at any rate, has invariably been the effect of the measure proposed, whenever it has aforetime been put into operation; and no other remedial policy has in any instance yet proved efficacious, in the same financial situation of affairs.

As matter of fact, gold does *not* necessarily flow into the country having the highest rate of interest; but into the country to which it is *owing*, and irrespective of the rate of interest there: and England has ever been the most eminent creditor country to the rest of the world ; gold ever flows into our ports in a perennial stream: the importation of bullion, during only the first ten months of the year, being as much as 24 millions sterling. .

It is, indeed, a great misfortune, that our financial writers should have treated this subject so theoretically, and not more practically ; because the latter, it seems to us, is the *only* manner in which the investigation can be usefully pursued.

Gold always procurable from abroad.

Our writers seem to regard *gold*, because it becomes the circulating medium, as possessing some mysterious property which completely isolates it from the category of other commercial commodities. And yet it is a fact, undisputed amongst practical men, that gold can be purchased, at any time, and in any country where it exists, just as cotton or corn can be obtained, by simply paying the cost; which, in regard to gold need seldom exceed some one or two per cent. of the value, to cover the charges of transport, &c. Need we say, that no such insignificant per centage of expense should be allowed to impede or prevent the maintenance of an adequate supply of gold to the Bank, when the consequences of its failure must prove so calamitous to the country. Indeed, were the expenses to be even *cent. per cent.*, upon the few millions of gold which, we have seen, constitute the whole basis of our commercial and industrial system; still, we ought gladly to incur it, to escape the infinitely more formidable tax of a 10 per cent. rate of interest, culminating in a disastrous national crisis!

It will not perhaps be disputed, however, that a merchant, who required gold from any foreign market in the world, for some commercial object to which the *expense* of procuring it was quite a secondary consideration, could, by simply offering in exchange some commodity of equivalent value, obtain gold *ad libitum*.

We know too, from experience, that any foreign Government, requiring gold for purposes of State, finds no difficulty whatever in taking away *ours*, by the sale or the hypothecation of securities, or by means of a temporary credit, which such foreign Government can always with facility arrange for, by simply paying the commission and charges incident to such an operation.

These, we say, are obviously *practical* methods of procuring gold. But the Bank of England, instead of taking any practical steps whatever, merely raises her rate, as if it were a magician's wand to conjure with; or rather, perhaps, seated, like Canute on the sea shore, she supinely waits for the laws of nature to obey her preposterous mandate!

Is it not matter of history, that on three memorable occasions, in 1847, 1857, and 1866, the Bank, in this manner, sat idly waiting for the expected effect, until the value of money was advanced to 10 and 12 per cent.; and gold, regardless all the time of that grave fact, steadily fell lower and lower at the Bank, until the Banking reserve was completely exhausted, and a state of general bankruptcy impended!

As the rule, a drain of gold occurs only in obedience to a *law of nature* in the commercial world. The attempt to arrest it is puerile: one might as well attempt to stay the efflux of the tides. It is not the *drain* which is at fault, but the *Bank;* who, while knowing her liability thereto in any year, *neglects all provision* against it. For this state of things the Government is responsible, and it is, indeed, high time the country woke up to protect itself against such wholesale and disastrous treachery towards the most vital interests of the nation.

Our argument, of course, is, that the merely raising the rate of interest, during any serious drain, is perfectly inoperative for the object designed; and we may doubtless challenge all controversy on this point, so long as we are able to appeal to *three* such fatally decisive and undisputed experiments as those just referred to. Upon these authoritive data, we without hesitation, further, say, that if the Bank, during the period of any future serious drain of gold, will simply despatch one of the Bank porters, with directions to *ply* incessantly the *handle* of *Aldgate Pump*, the effect will be far more beneficial, in every respect, than any policy she has yet tried, for the object contemplated.

In conclusion, we humbly submit, that the question under discussion, is one in regard to which the interests of the aggregate Public should be held *paramount* to those of the *merely Moneyed classes;* and that the Government, when dealing with so enormous a tax on the national industry, should decide between such a plutocracy and the community at large, the Government itself being, at least, a disinterested arbiter.

Should they undertake to do so, we must only adjure them to remember—that their decision has reference to the entire mass of the industrial and commercial capital of the country, represented by the astounding sum of £5,000,000,000 per annum, for one class only of its annual payments!—and that 4 per cent. additional interest thereon, is of the nature of a *tax* at the rate of some £16,000,000 per month, or £200,000,000 per annum!—a tax, too, which, under our necessarily artificial money system, it is in the power of the Government either to perpetuate, or remove.

Need we then repeat the opinion, that any Government, who shall deal successfully and satisfactorily with this great problem, will acquire an immortality of distinction which no other legislative success can by possibility confer : compared with which, all other fiscal, or social questions, sink into absolute insignificance ; and, in contributing our own quota of light to the important discussion, we simply suggest, as the manifest dictate of common sense, that the disastrous, but otherwise futile, expedient of raising the rate of interest, be at once abandoned for an opposite policy, of beneficial and more hopeful augury.

The Act of 1844, although chiefly promoted by Sir Robert Peel, it is pretty well understood, was framed also under the counsels of Mr. S. J. Lloyd, since created Lord Overstone.

What action did those counsels prescribe as the remedy for a drain of specie? In effect, the advice was simply *to enact a frightful money panic!*—to close our manufacturing establishments, *and throw the population* by hundreds of thousands *out of employment!* We do not wish to assert, that what we must designate a very malignant sort of counsel, was really the dictate of a mind in which every touch of humanity must have become extinct. But what we must and do maintain is, that no educated mind, which had not become the dupe of a theory, could have conceived or uttered counsels so fraught with wide spread calamity! The inevitable result of those counsels being carried into effect ought *of itself* to have produced the conviction, that any monetary system which could only be sustained by such support, was self condemned and worthy only of reprobation.

To the question (No. 2757) put by the Parliamentary Committee of 1840,—" Then if the drain arise from any special cause, such as an *importation of foreign corn*, do you think it would be reasonable, under such circumstances, in order to produce an effect on the Exchanges, *to cause a pressure?*" Mr. S. J. Lloyd's reply was, " Yes."

The " pressure" referred to being on " the prices of manufactures."

This word, " manufactures," embraces of course the entire productions of our national industry; and the " pressure" which Lord Overstone counsels being put upon them, was to be exerted by means of a violent " contraction" of the circulating medium, —which, up to the period of this interference, had been beneficently diffusing the blessings of thrift and happiness amongst the working population at large; and this was counselled, in order that the usual buyers of such productions in the various markets of the kingdom, should be *compelled,*—by their straitened means, and by the attendant universal panic and distrust of everything and everybody,—to *abstain from further purchases ;* until the producers,— unable to effect sales, and finding their property ruinously reduced in value, as the necessary consequences of such a state of things,—determine either temporarily or permanently, immediately to *contract* or *close* their works.

Now, this is the money panic, the creation which Lord Overstone, as we have seen, counsels, as the only means of preserving our money laws intact ! Let us for a moment consider its effects upon only one class of property,—that represented by our 5,000 millions of commercial Bills. One of the disastrous results of a money-panic is, to depreciate nearly every description of property, by some 30 per cent! What sum then must *one-third* of 5,000 millions amount to! The acceptors of these Bills have received, in exchange for them, an equivalent in various commodities, which they hoped to re-sell in time to meet duly their accept-ances; but, in the interval since they made those purchases, something has unexpectedly intervened, which has exerted a "*pressure*" upon their *value*, and has so produced a loss to their owners, of 1,000 to 2,000 millions sterling!

It is in this crisis of affairs, that the operation of the Act, which had produced it, has been three times suspended. The motive to the suspension was, in each instance, the realised imminence of impending national bankruptcy. That the appre-hension of such a grave catastrophe was not exaggerated,[*] must be evident from the fact, that provision had to be made by the acceptors, for the payment of over 100 millions of Bills weekly, which the acceptors had been rendered unable to provide for, through the impossibility of effecting their usual sales of goods, in consequence of the sudden and arbitrary contraction of the circulating medium: such contraction being the *avowed* object of an Act,

---

[*] The *Bankers' Magazine*, for November, 1847, records, that a deputation of merchants presented a memorial, which stated:—"Your Lordship may depend upon us when we assure you, that, if the present pressure be not relieved, merchants and other traders of undoubted respectability, who are not only solvent, but rich, and who have merchandise and bills which, under ordinary circumstances, would afford easy and ample means of meeting engagements, will inevitably be compelled to stop payment."

framed confessedly to enforce Lord Overstone's
humane edict, that, if a gold circulation chanced to
fail, *no other* should take its place, even if
commerce, as the result, became an impossibility !

The foregoing, indisputably, have been the results of this celebrated Act of Parliament,—framed as
being all that was needed to confer *perfection* on our
financial system ; and which, when introducing it,
Sir Robert Peel, in an eloquent exordium, described
as being designed,—" To inspire just confidence in
the medium of exchange, to put a check on improvi-
dent speculations, and to insure, so far as legislation can
insure, the just reward of industry, and the legitimate
profit of commercial enterprise, conducted with
integrity and controlled by provident calculation."

Instead of realizing those anticipations, it is this
same Act which, we have seen, constitutes the
climax of a most pernicious system ; and to the
suspension of which Act, when it had served only to
bring the country, within three years, to the very
verge of a general bankruptcy, *Sir Robert Peel
himself* gave his sanction.

The poet, Cowper, once sang of his country, as
as being the land,—

" Where power secures what industry has won ;
And to succeed, is not to be undone."

Had he lived in our times, he must rather, we
think, have lamented over its destiny, as being more
like the country scourged by the barbarities of a tyrant

like Genghis Khan, or that more modern Egyptian
despot,—

> · In whose fair lineaments none could trace
> The deeds that lurked within, and stained him with disgrace."

Had the Act in question frankly declared that it
was purposely designed, at intervals of every few
years, to *rob* industry of its fair reward, by the
seizure and confiscation of *one-third* of all its
productions, that description would still have fallen
short of the actual results.

The Act of 1844 was designed, among other
objects, to avert the possibility that the Bank
should fail to meet its engagements. And, doubtless,
the failure of such an institution would be an evil which
all must deplore. But, it is not possible, that even
that grave event is of a moment's consideration,
compared with the national and universal results of
so carrying out this Act that the acceptors of 5000
millions of bills should be actually compelled to stop
payment, by means, simply, of the operation of
a system which went directly in this way, to sacrifice
the *Nation* in order to save the *Bank!* We have
Railway Companies now, who are not only richer
and more extensive than the Bank; but whose
failure, were it possible to produce it, would
prove of equally serious consequence. On this head,
we may well observe, that it is no business of the
country to sustain the Bank. Let the Government itself take possession of the *Issue* department, and in
the other department let the Bank take care of her-

self; and stand or fall, like every other commercial concern, according as the management of her private affairs is successful, or otherwise. But let the *country* be *freed* from all concern about the issue ; and no longer be mixed up unnecessarily with the fate of the Bank, by means of an Act of Parliament which now involves equally the *Issue* Department, which alone is a *national* concern, in the success or failure of the other.

Now, we must here beg of the cotton manufacturers of Manchester and its vicinity,—to whose enterprise Lord Overstone, we know, was indebted for his great wealth,—to weigh well these felicitous counsels of this pre-eminent authority, and which have been since embodied in the Bank Act of 1844. Let our Yorkshire, Staffordshire, and our other great manufacturers, and the entire class of merchants, who hold the stocks of foreign productions needful for the supply of the kingdom—also meditate well upon the same counsels ; and remember that, *unless* all this national loss and suffering can be borne periodically, by every commercial and industrial interest, and by the population employed therein, this most direful consequence will happen,—*the Bank Charter Act cannot be upheld!!*

A sublime example, truly, of the " *Mons parturiens* " and the " *ridiculus Mus.*"

A man of science conceives the idea of an invention, and brings it to the test by means of an experiment ; but, finding the result to be an explosion which blows up the entire city, he is satisfied without further argument that it is a mistake, and abandons the brilliant idea. But *here*, we have an Act of Parliament which, after being three times brought to the *experimentum crucis*, has *three times* exploded; visiting unparalleled disasters upon the whole nation; and yet its authors are unconvinced; and the *Times* newspaper even *congratulates* us, that we are still blest with so wonderful a system of misrule and oppression, that its operation has *only* to be *suspended*, to afford universal relief!

The *modus operandi* of the Act,—by Col. Torrens.

This process of "contraction" is graphically described by another disciple of the same philosophical school—Col. Torrens, who says:—"By means of *contracting the circulation* the cash at the command of the Bankers and bill brokers being diminished, ⁰ ⁰ * ⁰ the merchants and dealers who employed Bankers, finding their cash balances reduced, and their accustomed amount of discounts diminished, would *abstain from purchases*, and from all those several causes *the prices of commodities would decline*, and the rate of interest advance."

The state of things so described, is, of course, nothing more or less than the operation of a money panic. It is an attack, in the first place, on that most vital circulation of commerce, amounting to some 5,000 millions of bills, representing chiefly the wholesale traffic of the kingdom:—for the object is by these authorities declared to be, to *contract the circulation, in order* that merchants and dealers should *abstain from purchases* and *so cause a fall of prices!*

Now, of this vast volume of bills, there are over 100 millions weekly, the payment of which has to be provided for by their acceptors. The acceptors have put their names to the bills, in trust that the natural course of markets will continue undisturbed, and afford the necessary opportunity to effect sales of their stocks, in time to realize from the proceeds sufficient means for the payment of their acceptances as they fall due. Need we here remark, that, without any such conspiracy by the financial classes—as that described by Col. Torrens —the acceptors of Bills have ordinarily, though exercising every foresight and pains, quite enough to do to make the due provision for them. What must it be then, if this formidable hostility of an all powerful institution, like the Bank of England, (which ought, indeed, to be the chief support of our commercial system), is thus set in motion to subvert its very foundations!

Need we say, that manufacturing establishments are set up, not for the object of keeping a few millions of gold in the Bank of England; but for the purpose of gaining a profit on the investment of their capital. If the *profit* fails, so does the *Concern.* Its doors are closed, and its workers turned adrift, deprived of the means of sustenance. In this way, not less probably than *thirty per cent.* of our entire labouring population, under the money

panic of 1847, were *deprived of a livelihood*. It was
then estimated that, in London alone more than
100,000 artisans were thus made to suffer hardships,
which, to men with dependent families, are necessarily one of the severest trials of life.° No wonder
that so many of these sufferers, disgusted with their
own country, should exile themselves to seek a
refuge in some foreign land. The loss of so many of
our skilled labourers, from this cause, is indeed
forcing attention upon what has already become a
great social problem; namely, how the various
industries of the country, on the return of more
prosperous times, can be maintained, when the
scarcity of hands to work them has become so
manifest.

It would obviously be a work of supererogation
to search for *other* causes to account for a money
panic, where this terrible engine of monetary " contraction " was known to have been put in operation.
Its *design* and its inevitable *effect* are manifestly to
produce the most formidable and universal of money
panics, and equally so whether *preceded* by *overtrading* or *not*.

Under its operation, bankruptcies *must be multiplied;* while, in many once *wealthy* concerns,

---

* " At a meeting, on the 27th March, of the delegates of the various trades of
the metropolis, the report of the Committee was read, the purport of which was
' that there were about 200,000 artisans and mechanics in the metropolis ; that one
third of them were employed, but about one half of the number had not remu-
nerating wages ; that another third were only occasionally employed ; and that the
remaining third were entirely dependant on parochial relief.' "— *Economist,
April, 1st.*

wounds and sores are established by fearful losses of
capital, which, though afterwards bolstered up for a
time, must eventually break out in disaster, when
and where perhaps least expected.
Our money system is, besides, the great *nursery*
of *overtrading*. It permits money to fall so low as
one per cent., and to become a "*drug*." It then
forces out loans of low-priced capital; but no sooner
has its credulous victim embarked in some tempting
undertaking, than this overwhelming engine of
"contraction" falls ruthlessly upon him, and, by
ruinous rates of interest takes all he has, and scatters
to the winds his promising enterprise.

Lord Overstone, before the Committee of 1840, *The Rule, that Currencies must conform to Gold.*
gave it as his opinion, that any substitute for gold
that may be adopted as a circulating medium—and
which substitute he considered Bank paper to be,—
ought to be made to follow precisely the same
variations in quantity, as would happen if it were
not paper at all, but had remained entirely of gold.
That, consequently, if the gold in the Bank, of which
the paper was held to be only the representative,
should from any cause diminish in quantity, the
paper should be forcibly, and, in the same degree,
contracted also.
Now, this rule is of the greatest importance in *The theory of "Contraction."*
this discussion, because it constitutes the *funda-
mental* law of our present money system. There
can be no mistake as to its meaning: If the country

E

should be unable to procure *gold* for its circulating medium, it is to *contract* or *abolish* entirely, as the case may be, the *substitute* for gold; and the national industries, dependent necessarily on a medium of exchange, are to be closed; or else the country must return to the state of barter! Obviously, such are the sole alternatives involved in the enforcement of so insane a law!

This, then, is the strange and cruel law which the Act of 1844 was invented to enforce upon the country. On three memorable occasions, we have already seen, the law was applied, until its effects had passed all endurance; when this contraction of the circulating medium was demonstrated to be a signal failure, and the Act which enforced it was accordingly suspended.

Is it possible, let us ask, that any man, capable of looking to the consequences of a policy, could tender counsel like this?

Now, it so happened to this country, in the year 1797, and to the United States, in the year 1861, that *gold entirely failed* to supply an adequate circulating medium: And we put to the reader the question, whether our own country, rather than prosecute the great war with the first Napoleon to a successful issue; or, the United States, rather than she should have maintained her civil contest until its object was gained,—whether, we say, both countries *ought* to have *abandoned* the struggle at the outset, upon such advice as that tendered by

Lord Overstone; because, simply, the gold currency could not yield the necessary sinews of war; or, whether both countries ought not rather, setting aside such sage counsels, to have acted just as they wisely determined to do, namely, to *invent*, as a substitute for gold, a *paper* currency; which not only answered every purpose of commerce, but enabled both countries to accomplish, to the fullest extent, the object for which gold had been found inadequate? Only one answer, of course, can be given to these questions.

We have no wish certainly, to speak disrespectfully of such an authority as Lord Overstone; yet, with regard to such a rule as that now under consideration, we cannot conceive how it would be possible to crowd into a single sentence a greater amount of infatuation and hurtful folly!

This rule, of course, assumes it to be a *law of nature*, although contrary to extant facts, that gold and silver *alone* are *money*. Let us, therefore, for a moment assume that this rule of conforming the paper currency to the movements and to the standard of gold or silver, is possible. *What Age* of the world, we ask, are we to select to ascertain and verify the true standard? The earliest age in which history records the use of gold and silver money, we presume, is that of the patriarch Abraham: Is it of that age we are to adopt the standard? Alas! who shall assure us of the relative value of gold to other commodities in that remote period? Ought we then to adopt the standard which obtained in the age of the *Cæsars*, when it seems the Roman *penny* was equivalent to a *day's wages?* Or, are we to take that of our own country a few centuries back, when a *few pence* were the equivalent value of a fat *sheep?* Or, are we, in these modern times, to restore again the value of the pound sterling to its *original* quality and obvious meaning, namely, a *pound weight* of silver? Or, will the advocates of conformity, indeed, fall so low as to be content with the present *debased* and *depreciated* standard, of less than *four ounces* of silver to the pound sterling? This is *all* indeed they ask for, but such contentment on their part, with so debased a standard, seems only to demonstrate the utter absurdity and impracticability of the rule they contend for.*

The rule is a simple *impossibility*; or, why, in framing the Act of 1844 itself, was it so flagrantly

---

* "An Essay on Money," by John Taylor, states, page 69, that the Pound Weight of Silver :—

		A.D.			£		
1.	William I.	1066	was coined into		£1	0	0
28.	Edward I.	1300	"	"	1	0	3
18.	" III.	1344	"	"	1	2	6
25.	"	1351	"	"	1	5	0
13.	Henry IV.	1412	"	"	1	10	0
4.	Edward IV.	1467	"	"	1	17	6
18.	Henry VIII.	1527	"	"	2	5	0
34.	"	1543	"	"	2	10	0
36.	"	1545	"	"	4	16	0
37.	"	1546	"	"	7	4	0
4.	Edward VI.	1550	"	"	14	8	0
6.	"	1552	"	"	3	5	0
4.	Elizabeth	1562	"	"	3	0	0
43.	"	1601	"	"	3	2	0
56.	George III.	1816	"	"	3	6	0

violated? Does the permission which this Act gives to the Bank, to issue *fourteen millions* of paper *having no gold basis for it whatever*,—make the paper substitute to conform to the amount of gold it is said to represent! And why violate so fundamental a rule, in the very Act which, to the public, was designed chiefly to carry this rule into effect? The answer is a very simple one: the thing was an impossibility; the forcing the country, so to speak, into a metallic coat *so obviously* too contracted, was too palpably absurd even for the admirers of the rule to attempt.

But on what pretence, we may enquire, could such a vicious rule have ever been propounded? Because, forsooth, it is *assumed*, that nothing but *gold* or *silver* can give *value* to a circulating medium. We are relieved from the trouble of arguing this point, since we can appeal to the paper money of America, and of our own country, during the periods to which we have already referred. The history of these purely paper currencies, demonstrates the falsity of such an assumption.

We submit, that it is not gold that *imparts* value to the circulating medium: on the contrary, it is the adoption, by the legislature, of gold for that purpose, which *invests* gold with all the value it can possibly possess as a *circulating medium*. As a *commodity*, gold, like other commodities, has a value peculiar to itself; but, as a *currency*, it can have no value until it receives, in that capacity, the *sanction of the legislature;* which coins it, and declares the *weight* and *value* which must be *affixed* to each coin ; and this alone it is which gives currency to gold or silver as the circulating medium. Moreover, too, the same currency value which the legislature can confer on *gold*, it can give also to *any other* commodity it may prefer for use as money.

So far from its being true, as maintained by the upholders of the present money laws, that it is *gold* which gives *value* to a currency ; the contrary may readily be ascertained to be the fact, namely, that it is simply the *legislative sanction* given to gold which imparts to it all its value as the circulating medium. Thus, let it be supposed that all the nations of Europe were to deduce, from the American example now in operation, that a good, sufficient and more effective currency can be constituted by the legislature of any country,—without the aid of either gold or silver,—by a simple decree of such legislature that a mere piece of paper, duly stamped and authorised by the Government, shall be legal tender in all payments. And let such European Governments, including our own, satisfied and confident as to its efficacy,—from the wonderful results of the American experiment,—henceforth adopt such a currency, to the *exclusion* of gold and silver ;—What, we ask, would be the value of the precious metals under such new and altered circumstances ? It must be manifest that, being now discarded from their *principal* use, as money, and being left to find their value for other purposes, they must, so to speak, henceforth become a "drug" in the market, and of very reduced and uncertain value. Therefore, we maintain that gold is indebted for its present high value solely to legislative *decrees* which have *fixed* its value; and that the withdrawment of such artificially created value, by henceforth discharging gold from its present functions as money, would at once cause it necessarily to lose all such *money* value whatever. Further, this view of the case seems to us conclusive, as to the utter absurdity of Lord Overstone's rule, that *paper* money ought to *conform* to some fanciful effects of an assumed movement and standard of gold.

Anciently, we know, gold and silver were, for convenience, adopted generally as the money medium : their small bulk, in comparison with their value, seeming better than anything else, to fit them for use as a currency : *credit* money, in the form of bank notes, being in those earlier times, of course, quite unknown. Gold and silver, traditionally, come down to us, therefore, with this general prejudice in their favour, that they were the only medium of exchange known to our forefathers; and in semi-barbarous countries, and, we may add, in those only, they still continue to be used exclusively as money.

The value of gold and silver, as a currency, was derived originally, and still exists, in consequence simply of the adoption of them by the State, as legal money; and the value, so derived, would no longer exist, were the State to adopt another commodity, and transfer to such commodity the money value which had previously been legally *fixed* and *stamped* upon gold and silver.

With regard to a *domestic* currency, this is certainly the case ; but, so far as respects *international* exchanges, until some other international medium shall be substituted for the precious metals, the *balance of trade* must continue, as now, to be paid only in those commodities.

Within a century or two only, before paper money was known in England, the country, as we have lately seen is the case with France at this day, abounded in private hoards of gold and silver ; from which stores, when any large portion of the active circulation was drained away abroad, the vacuum was readily filled up.

No such private hoards, however, now exist, since the distribution of Banks at all points. The Banks now at once absorb all unemployed gold and silver, as well as Bank notes, and the provincial Banks again pass their own surplus money to the Bank of England ; which institution may, therefore, now be said to contain *the whole unemployed*, uninvested capital of the country ; and the *aggregate* of this capital must always be limited, therefore, to the Reserve of Bank notes in the Banking Department. Now it is to this *surplus* of money capital, that the process of " contraction " is so fatally directed, and which capital, that fearful process, if not **arrested**, would either contract or extinguish !

Further, with regard to this assumption, that *gold* only can confer value on the circulating medium : We wish those who impute this power to gold, would ponder the following question : How it happens, that £100 of three per cent. Consols is, in our day, worth so nearly *par*, in our so-called *gold* currency ; when, under the Bank Restriction Act, the same £100 stock was worth little more than *half* its present value, and that in *inconvertible paper*? During the period referred to, it is matter of history, that a purely paper currency really purchased £100 of Consols, for about half the price which has since been paid for it in *gold!* And those who believe that gold *only* can give value to a currency, we apprehend, must be puzzled to find any principle on which our question can be answered.

But lay aside the *assumption*, and the answer is obvious : During the earlier period, the *rate of interest* on the paper issues of the Bank was permanently maintained at *five* per cent., the Usury Laws alone preventing its rising higher; but since the return to specie payments, the normal Bank rate has been only about *three* per cent. It must be very obvious, that a *three* per cent. stock, with money at *three* per cent., must intrinsically, so to speak, be worth nearly £100; and that with interest at *five* per cent., a three per cent. stock could not be worth more than £50 or £60 : For any property, calculated to yield with certainty *five* per cent. return per annum, must be worth more, *pro rata*, than the same property would be if yielding only *thi ee* per cent. per annum : because a £1,000 invested in such property, would yield £50 per annum at five per cent., and only £30 per annum if returning not more than *three* per cent. per annum.

Money which is worth *five* per cent. per annum, must always be equal in value to every other kind of property, also yielding five per cent. per annum; and £100, with interest at *three* per cent., is of exactly equal value to £100 value of other property also yielding three per cent. ; and, therefore, £~~100~~ 60 with interest at *five* per cent., is of equal value to only £~~60~~ 100 value of any property yielding only three per cent.

It is thus plainly to be seen, that it is the *interest* value which money bears, and not *gold* which must constitute it the *standard* of value to all property, the value of which is estimated by the rate of its annual return.

It is *not* gold which gives value to the currency; otherwise, three per cent. Consols should have been of the greater value, when estimated in an *inconvertible* currency, than they now are worth, estimated in a *gold* currency.

And here we have a practical illustration how a *gold* currency, if inflation can be alleged, may *inflate* prices; because it has given to Consols so much higher value than they were able to attain in merely inconvertible paper, by 30 to 40 per cent.!

It results from this, that, had our Government,

when, during the last French war, they contracted the principal portion of our National Debt, required the Bank to issue her inconvertible paper at *three* per cent. instead of five per cent.; and so maintained the value of money normally at about the former rate, they would have received, for each £100 of three per cent. consols, nearly £100,—instead of only £50 to £60, for every £100 of such stock! The consequence would obviously have been that, as they would have received nearly £2 for £1 actually paid to them, the National Debt must have been *less*, by *nearly half*, than the 800 millions, at which it now stands: and the taxes, annually imposed upon the country to provide for the interest upon the debt, would also have been *less* than they are, by *one half* also: To this important consideration, we must respectfully beg the attention of the Chancellor of the Exchequer, on the next occasion, when he may be called upon to prepare the sinews for a great war.

In maintaining as we do, that it is in the power of the *legislature* to *regulate* the *rate of interest*, we are not presenting any debateable proposition, but one which must be self evident. Because any legislature or institution which held the sole control over the *quantity* of any commodity, must, for that reason, equally possess control over its *value* or price.

It should, therefore, be very evident, we think, that the *rate* of interest really wields this extraordinary power—that it becomes, necessarily, not only the *standard*, but also the *regulator* of value to every description of Fixed property whatsoever.

From this *natural law* of the case, we may therefore safely draw the important practical conclusion—that the *rate* of interest must ever *govern*,—that is, must stimulate or restrict the amount of capital that can be profitably applied to great industrial undertakings, and to the creation of new works of public utility : for example, the construction of railways, the improvement of land, or the extension of manufactories over the country. For, how *many* of such investments must necessarily yield a satisfactory return, if the capital invested therein cost only three per cent.; and how very *few* indeed, in this country, if the rate of interest were permanently maintained at ten per cent.

And yet our financial economists persist in acting just as though the *law* of the case were precisely the *reverse* of the canon we have now deduced. *They* upheld the rate of interest at *five* per cent. during the last great war, when it was equally in the power of the Bank to have reduced the rate to *three* per cent.; the consequence of so grave a mistake being, that these high authorities have bequeathed to posterity a national debt of some 300 or 400 millions—with taxation in proportion — *more than was necessary*, except for their great misconception of the whole case, which dictated the injurious policy then adopted.

Biassed by the same perversion of views, the

late Sir Robert Peel also, when the money panic of
1847 had reached its climax—alarmed at the
danger which threatened the country unless the Act
of 1844 should be suspended—consented to such
suspension; but, at the same time, coupling with
the relief so afforded, the arbitrary condition,
that the Bank should not issue its paper at any
lower rate of interest than *eight* per cent.!

We entirely demur therefore to the assumption,
that gold is necessary to give to a currency its
money value, or its purchasing power: and, on the
contrary, we maintain, upon the facts just cited,
that the value of the circulating medium, be it gold
or paper, is to be measured solely by the *rate* of
interest it will command, as money; and that the
rate of interest is regulated solely by the *quantity* of
such money, with reference to the demand for its use!

With the greatest deference we would here
remark, that this, perhaps, is not one of that large majority of questions that may be left to be decided by
a newspaper press. The editorial staff is necessarily
composed of literary men, whose views on a subject
like this, would rather be *theoretical* than practical;
derived possibly from those very few authorities, so
called, who may be consulted by the student.*

---

* Having ourselves carefully read, as well as tested by an experience and
observation of nearly thirty years, most that has been written on this subject; we
beg to refer the reader, for the most valuable, perhaps the only *practical* information, from every side of the discussion, to be obtained thereupon,—to the ample
Reports of the Lords', and of the Commons' Committees, on the Distress of 1847
the Report of the Parliamentary Committee of 1840; and that of the Bullion
Committee of 1811.

And certainly the question is not one that may fairly be left to the decision of the great *Moneyed class;* whose interests in the matter are so diametrically opposed to those of the community at large. It might be more safely left, we think, to those whose daily pursuits and avocations enable them to *feel*, as well as thoroughly to understand the question in all its most important bearings: that is, to those *Mercantile* and *Manufacturing* classes, whose enterprise and capital originate and sustain the vast industrial activity of the nation; from which alone, directly or indirectly, the entire community, from *peer* to *peasant*, derive their entire income and subsistence.

Now we must observe that, although the strange counsel offered by Lord Overstone, while it was in operation, was, as we have seen, equivalent to the worst possible *malediction* he could have bestowed upon his country,—to *himself* the effect was doubtless otherwise; because, an advance of the rate of discount from 3 to 12 per cent. must necessarily have the effect of *quadrupling the profits* of a *discounting* business !

To us, this inevitable result of counsel so given, is palpable enough: for it is simply as if a guild of *Farmers* or *Millers*, possessing the ear of legislature, should strenuously urge for and obtain an Act of the legislature, which should forthwith raise the *price* of *bread* to their customers, to a point that would quadruple the profits of their business : and this on some theoretic though transparent plea, that it was a measure designed only for *the public good!*

Such considerations, however, seem to us to take the question entirely out of the category of *Political Economy* problems, and to reduce it simply to one of *commercial fairness and morality.*

We hope to establish beyond question the truth of our position,—that it belongs to the *legislature alone* to deal with all matters relating to the *currency,* the legislature consulting only the advantage of the community at large. The Legislature's power over the Currency.

The upholders of our existing money laws, on the contrary, maintain—and, doubtless, many commercial men also imagine,—that money simply resembles every commercial commodity in this respect; that it should be left to find its own value, under the law of Supply and Demand. Accordingly, and as a practical corollary to the existing money system, the *Usury* Laws have been *repealed* in modern times, to admit of money dealers obtaining for its use as *high a rate of interest as they can command.*

Obviously, this proposition in regard to money, *assumes* that money really is, in this view, situated like any other commercial commodity; and if the proposition were *proved* instead of *assumed* merely, that such is the actual situation of money, we could have nothing to say in support of the opposite rule.

What then are the *facts?* A merchant imports a cargo of *Wheat* from California. When it is shipped, he can have no knowledge, of course, of what price it will command on its arrival in England, in some four months time afterwards ; but he must run the *risk* of its either realising perhaps twenty per cent. *loss,* or it may be gaining twenty per cent. *profit !*

Now, let him ship in the same vessel a ton weight of *Gold.* Is the gold *at all* in the same situation as the cargo of wheat ? The latter commodity, wheat, takes the chance of the market price, whatever it may be, on its arrival. But for the *gold* the shipper *knows absolutely,* when the shipment is made, the *exact price* he will receive for every ounce of it, arrive when it may in England.

This point the legislature has determined for him beforehand, by fixing a price of £3 17s. 10½d. per ounce, at which rate the Bank is *obliged by law* to give him for it the current money of the country. The Bank cannot give him a *higher* price, and the importer has no need to take for it elsewhere any *lower* price. Thus the price and value are fixed absolutely for the gold. The merchant therefore cannot help making a *profit* on the gold, if he should have bought it in California at a lower price than £3 17s. 10½d. per ounce. But, as respects the *wheat,* although he had purchased that commodity at even *twenty* per cent. below its value at the place of shipment, all is *uncertain* as to profit and loss. He might find the price in England, on its arrival there, fallen so low as to cause him a *loss* of even twenty per cent.

Then, we ask, *is* gold, as assumed by our opponents, situated at all like wheat, or any other commercial commodity? Certainly not. The legislature, before admitting gold as the currency, exercised its right of fixing only *one* price at which it should circulate. Is there any other commodity so situated? What then becomes of the rule, so manifestly based on the false assumption, that *money* is situated like *other* commodities? It is not so certainly: inasmuch as the *legislature* has exercised its right to *declare* the *only price* at which *gold* shall be exchanged.

Money differs essentially from other commodities again, in this respect, that the holders have no control over the *supply*, and, therefore, can have no claim to dictate its *price*. The legislature, we know, claims and exercises this right over the currency of the country, by regulating its amount. It has absolutely decreed that the currency shall consist of £14,000,000 of *Bank notes*, which have *no relation whatever to gold or silver:* And the latter commodities *alone*, we know, are *money* in the estimation of our opponents. It was equally in the power of the legislature, of course, to have declared, that there should be no *Bank note* currency whatever; or, it might have decreed that *gold* itself should *no longer* constitute any portion of the currency. Suppose, therefore, that the legislature had so *excluded gold* from the currency, *what*, we ask, would then have been the *value of gold* to the holder?

On these matters of *fact* then, we found our

F

rule, that the legislature has the exclusive right to
say *what medium* shall constitute the currency of
the country; that it has also the power, as we
have seen, to *regulate its quantity;* that it has
already *fixed the price* of gold as a commodity; and
that it has, therefore, the same power to fix the
rate of interest at any point it may deem best, as
it also undoubtedly had to enact, or to repeal, the
Usury Laws.

We think there cannot remain a doubt on this
point: and therefore we see nothing whatever
defensible in the objection to our plan, that money-
dealers alone have the right to regulate the rate of
interest. This power of the legislature over the
rate of interest has not only been *exercised*; but,
unfortunately for the country, has *ever* been exercised for the advantage *solely* of the *money-dealers:*
Such was the case under the Bank Restriction
Act, when for 20 years the rate of interest was
maintained at so needlessly high a rate as *five* per
cent. It was for the benefit of the same class that
the Usury Laws were repealed; and it has invariably been the same also whenever the Bank Act
of 1844 has been suspended : The rate seems always
unfortunately to have been fixed by the Government,
on such occasions, at as *high a point as possible!*
Would that on any future similar occasion, the
Government, when exercising such powers, might
be influenced exclusively by considerations of what
would manifestly most conduce to the *public good.*

Were our legislature, therefore, acting on their undoubted *right*, to issue a National Currency in just such *quantity* as would serve to maintain the rate of interest at that point which should be found to be the *average* rate at the Bank of England since the return to cash payments,—that is, at about three per cent.,—the interest value of the *circulating medium* would thus be *fairly* so fixed or regulated : But after thus regulating the value of *money* at its source of issue, let every *capitalist* be at liberty to obtain, for the loan of his *capital*, any rate of interest whatever, which such capital would command in the market. In this way, the value of *money* would be fixed by the *legislature ;* but the value of *capital*, which is, of course, quite another matter, would be left to adjust itself between its owners and borrowers, under the law of Supply and Demand.

The practical conclusion then forced upon ourselves by this investigation is, that our monetary system, from first to last, *since* and *before* the enactment of the Law of 1844, has been demonstrated to be a *failure*.

For our immense commercial fabric has been made to rest upon the *prudence* of the Bank of England, as to the preservation, or loss, of a *very few* millions of gold : rewarding her, however, not for the exercise of that prudence, but in the exact ratio in which she has *abandoned* it !

A fabric so upraised could not, by possibility, have encountered any other than the fate, which,

as a natural consequence of resting upon so inadequate a foundation, has periodically overtaken and
subverted it.

We are unable to conceive how a remedy is to
provided, except it be, *in principle at least*, identical
with that advocated in these pages, namely :

1st.—To transform the present *Issue* Department of the Bank of England into a *Government*
Department for the issue of a National currency, to
supersede that of the Bank now in circulation. This
must give a *National dignity* and *security* to the
currency, to which no other could of course pretend.

2nd.—To make *visible* and *certain* provision
for the convertibility into gold of such National
paper, by means of an office to be opened in the
proposed new Bank of Issue, and to be charged
with the responsibility of providing a special supply
of foreign gold, in anticipation of any special drain
which should impend on the Bank; and that the
said office be equipped for the purpose, and
furnished with the needful basis for the operation,
by holding at all times an adequate amount of
undoubted Foreign Funds; to be sold and converted
into gold abroad, whenever occasion should demand
the necessary supply of bullion to the Bank; in
order to enable the Bank to maintain the convertibility of its paper, without recourse to *advanced
rates of interest* for such an object.

Until the public common sense shall take up

this great question in a *practical* manner, and—deducing from the experiments so long tried, and fully ascertained to have been disastrous failures, shall determine to enter upon practical experiments of a diametrically opposite character and tendency—little, we fear, need be hoped for in the shape of a needful Reform of our monetary system : For we seem to be in the same position as that in which the Scientific world stood, prior to the overthrow of those renowned schools of *theoretic* philosophy which preceded the establishment- of the Baconian system. Whether or not the world, in our day, be capable of furnishing another *Bacon*, with powers equal to the undertaking, who shall, on the subject under discussion, be successful in superseding the *fanciful* by the *practical*, time must reveal. But we confess, it strikes us very forcibly, as a matter of surprise, that in an age distinguished, as the present has been, by so many grand and useful scientific discoveries : in regard to this important department of inquiry.—before which the majority of social problems sink into such insignificance, an enquiry too which has challenged and baffled the skill of the eminent names who have so long led public opinion on this subject,—nothing whatever should yet have been accomplished to protect the commerce and industry of the country from the visitation of the most fearful of national scourges : scourges induced too, by means of what was certainly intended to be, and as certainly, we think, might be constituted, the unfailing and most effective *boon* and blessing to mankind universally.

It has been our aim, throughout these pages, to advance no *uncertain* position, to deduce no conclusion, but such as will stand the test of that infallible touchstone of true science, namely, *Experience.*

Doubtless, all true science, all *certain* truth, must have been derived solely from *Experience:* From our *own* experience, or the experience of *others* credibly conveyed to us. In science, so derived, and in no other, is there absolute *certainty.* Beyond the domain of actual experience, all is chaos,—the *terra incognita* of mere speculation, and dubious, baseless, *opinion.*

Probability merely, however strong, is not *certainty,* and, therefore, is no part of *Science;* whose simple definition is the knowledge of *ascertained facts.* The greater portion of human projects must, in the first instance, proceed on probability alone ; but nothing except the carrying such projects into *practice,* and so reducing them to *experience,* can ascertain whether the probability be true or false. All *scientific* probability also, until so verified, is necessarily unreliable and valueless.

Our own *experience* of a fact is *certain* knowledge : we *know* that fire *burns,* for we have experimented, and ascertained the fact. We *believe* that such a country as China exists, having *credibly* learned from those who have visited it that such is the fact. Of the *invisible* world, we, and the wisest of mankind alike, *know* absolutely *nothing :* having had no *experience* of it whatever. We, notwithstanding, *believe*, with absolute certainty, everything made known to us respecting it, on the *credible* testimony of an accredited eye-witness, the Divine Christ. If this infallible dividing line of *experience* were universally applied as the *test* of scientific truth, to distinguish it from scientific fiction, what havoc must so inexorable a law make amongst those thousand crudities of scientific authorities ; which seem, indeed, to serve no other purpose than to show how eminent a fool a *wise* man may make of himself ; and upon how *slender* a basis of facts a huge superstructure of hypothesis and absurdity may be cleverly erected. Truly, Mr. Disraeli never uttered a truer judgment than when he declared that he would not pronounce the present age to be one of scientific progress, he should rather call it one of " *craven credulity.*"

The domain of true science is totally diverse from that of scientific *conjecture*. The former alone is truth, the latter is utterly baseless. It is only from this latter region of ignorance and presumption, that our *Bible* knowledge has been of late so confidently assailed : *never* from the former. The contents of a *Divine* record being absolute truth, must ever be in harmony with all true discoveries in science. Witness the ancient, incontestible stone tablets from Nineveh, Babylon, and Moab ! How signally indeed, do these confound the superficial criticisms of even a Bunsen, and other such authorities!

To learn how needful it is to receive nothing as scientific truth, which has not *experience* for its basis, let us ask what to-day is the situation of even Astronomical science,––of the sublime Newtonian theory? That theory was at first, we know, a mere *guess*, on the part of its author. The subsequent verifications of it, so called, have simply added to it a few degrees of *probability*. They are not in any sense *demonstrations*. The whole theory, as we know, rests upon two grand *assumptions*, which, in the nature of things, must ever be incapable of *demonstration:* namely, the *Earth's motion*, and the absence of a *resisting medium* in Space. To the former of these astronomical postulates, the distinguished astronomer Tycho Brahe, although the associate of Kepler,—as well as our immortal Bacon,—never saw sufficient evidence to demand their assent. To the latter position, objections, involving the very foundations of this great astronomical system, were recently urged by numerous members of the French Academy of Sciences; who held, with the astronomer Encke, that the existence of a resisting medium, was now *demonstrated*, by the observations of Donati's and other *Comets*.

If such then be the situation of even this most advanced and most exact of all the sciences, what may yet be the fate, as a consequence of the progressive march of truth, of those scientific phantasies which now mark and disfigure the scientific brochures of the present age!

What may yet be the fate of even those fanciful *Geological* canons of the "infallible *Stone-leaved Book*,"—which *progressive research* is now so constantly overturning; while, for example, bringing up from the Ocean's depths *alive* myriads of "*extinct*" races; and revealing formations *in actual process now*, although such were assigned only to periods many *millions* of ages past! The Fauna and Flora, separated till lately by innumerable ages, are now found together in *one stratum*. The *Azoic* Old Red Sandstone, and, yet more startling, the *Azoic, Plutonic Granite*, also, now both of them abound in organic forms; while remains of the *Mastodon* and of *Man*, separated likewise, of course, by countless periods, are now discovered in one and the same alluvial bed.

Truly, a *sceptic* in this haughtiest of the Speculative Sciences, has at least *some* warrant for the conclusion : "If only twenty years' research has sufficed to demolish one *half* of this incontestible *Stone-Book;* how many years more may serve for the remaining half,—to throw aside indeed the *whole volume*, into the already overcrowded limbo of *pretended* and *exploded* sciences !

Looking simply to the latest Geological *Experience*, a professor of this vaunted Science would display equal temerity and credulity, who should now venture to deny that, at no very distant period, *every variety* of organic remains, which geological canons have till now separated by such vast periods of time, may yet be found deposited together in *one single stratum!*

If, then, these latest discoveries point so manifestly in that direction, would it not be more creditable to those professors of the Science who value a scientific reputation, to *abstain,* in future, from all merely sensational stories, with which in their too palpable weakness for the marvellous, they have so frequently astonished their gobemouche and credulous audiences : stories in which the Lecturer pretends to assign the various *ages,* as well as the *causes ;* and the *circumstances* under which the present crust of the Earth was deposited and formed ; as if indeed these were at all matters that could ever fall within the range of any merely human knowledge.

The intellectual world, doubtless, seems to stand in much need of, and to be now quite ripe for, the application of another *Novum Organum Scientiarum.* Some inexorable Law, which, applied like a Preceptor's Birch to the degenerate Literati of the great World of Letters, should henceforth establish—" wide as the Poles asunder "—a gulf of separation between True Science and its dogmatic Counterfeit : which should effectually distinguish the *Wheat* from the *Chaff;* ascertained *Facts* from mere *Theory; Experience* from *Conjecture;* and demonstrable *Science* from arrogant, presumptuous *Ignorance.*

The number of works of real Scientific worth, would doubtless thus be found to be very few indeed, compared with the voluminous, tinsel, and valueless productions of fictitious Science. But the former would contain *all* the pure unalloyed *Gold* of *Truth* we can possibly possess; and this would constitute their priceless Literary Distinction and practical Value.

We repeat then, that we have appealed only to well known and decisive *experiments*, to certify the truth of our conclusions; and we therefrom venture to assert, that if the eminent authorities who are opposed to us, will only in this respect follow our example, they cannot fail, we think, to arrive at similar results.

The Proposed Reform, the suggestion of Experience.

CONCLUSION.

We must now respectfully submit, that our argument fairly conducts to the following practical conclusions, namely:—

Analysis of the suggested Reform.

1st—That a money-panic is the most formidable visitation to which a great commercial nation can be subjected; contracting or destroying as it does the *means of subsistence* to the population at large; and, by throwing the industrial classes into a state of want and desperation, tends directly to the dissolution of all those civil and social bonds by which a nation is held together.

2nd.—That, a system of *Barter* in a civilised country being an impossibility, it becomes a most sacred duty of the legislature, to mature and sanction a monetary system, which shall at least be free from the disastrous results referred to, and which shall also admit of *steadiness*, and *expansibility* with the growing requirements of the national prosperity.

3rd.—Rejecting, therefore, the *dicta* of the ancient schoolmen, and of their modern disciples,— which demand that *facts* shall be made to conform to *theory*, and not theory to facts; in other words, which assert that the national industry and commerce should be made arbitrarily to *contract*, within the varying limits of an unsecured, uncertain, and ever fluctuating circulating medium;—we propose that the latter shall be so constituted as naturally to *adapt itself* to the expanding wants of the former; and that, in fact, this essential garment, so to speak, should be made to *fit the wearer*, and not the wearer cut down to the insufficient proportions of the garment.

4th.—That, since no commercial disorder, be it what it may, is capable of producing evils of one-thousandth part the magnitude of those produced by the barbarous expedient of a *violent contraction of* the *circulation*, now periodically resorted to as a remedy: That this remedy,—so much more fatal than the alleged disease itself—be, therefore, reprobated and abandoned ; and, in lieu thereof, that some more natural provision against the recurring exigency of a drain of gold, be immediately devised and adopted.

5th—That, on the lapse of the present Bank Charter, a National Issue of paper should supersede the present private issues of the Bank; and that, if need be, the agency of the present *Issue* Department of the Bank, be constituted a *Government* Department for the proposed new issue : That the country by this means, be furnished with a currency possessing the National security, and requiring, of course, no other *basis*.

6th.—That, in order to provide a permanent store of bullion, free from reduction during any future drain, and so to ensure permanently the convertibility of the national paper into *gold* ; the Government be empowered to issue a sufficient amount of 3 per cent. Consols, the proceeds of which shall be invested in good Foreign and interest-bearing Funds ; to serve, by their conversion into gold, for import from abroad,—not to *prevent* an impending drain,—but to *replace it*, by fresh supplies while in process : The interest accruing on the foreign funds, meanwhile, more than recouping any loss on the new issue of Consols.

7th.—Having provided, by means of this *forethought*,—what the present expedient of raising the rate of interest has ever failed to effect,—namely, such a contingent reserve of gold as would render unnecessary any higher rate of interest than the average rate of three per cent.; that now, further, the rate of interest be also prevented from falling *below* three per cent.,—at such times as the gold reserve becomes unnecessarily large, and consequently the rate of interest tends downwards to too low a point,—by means of a corrective such as the following : The Bank,—on observing the rate outside the Bank to tend to any *lower* point,—simply refusing to issue any *additional* paper in such circumstances ; but, on the contrary, making sales of a portion of its securities in order to *take up* any apparent excess of circulation.

8th.—That a National currency, so protected against danger of inconvertibility ; and the rate of interest, by the means proposed, being secured against needless variations, would necessarily supply the desideratum sought for,—namely, an adequate reform of the existing monetary system : The latter affording no such protection or security.

9th.—That, pending the current Charter of the Bank, and unless, by arrangement between the Government and the Bank, the plan proposed can be sooner introduced ; the Bank be required by legislative *mandate*, and by such means as are in her power, to maintain her store of gold at such an amount as will prevent the necessity of raising the rate of interest to a higher point than 3 per cent., and this on pain of the Bank's forfeiting her Charter : Or, failing such legislative injunction, that the *Government it-self* enter into immediate arrangements with the Messrs. Rothschild, to provide, through that agency, in the manner suggested, an available reserve of gold abroad, to be transferred to the Bank during any future drain: The Government issuing, as a basis for the operation, an adequate amount of three per cent. Consols.

10th.—That, with reference to the circumstances which are alleged to have rendered necessary the present 7 per cent. rate of interest, the Bank be *prohibited*, should the drain be protracted, from enacting any policy different from that sanctioned by the late *Sir Robert Peel himself*, during the crisis of 1847 : namely, from charging any *higher* rate than 8 per cent., on any plea whatever.

The suggestions we have ventured to offer, by no means point to the *only* plan of reform adequate to meet the case., Whatever plan will, on the one hand, secure to the community a steady, adequate circulating medium, at a moderate and equable rate of interest ; and, on the other, provide for the maintenance of a sufficient equable store of bullion in the Bank of Issue,—will equally suffice for every object.

Therefore, the following method, also, securing, as it does, both of those essential conditions, may appear to some even more simple in its application and operation than that before proposed.

A second method of Reform.

To illustrate, therefore, a *second* method of dealing with our problem, assume, in the first place, that there are in general circulation some 80 to 100 millions of *specie*; that there are also in the Bank some 20 millions of *bullion*; and that these, with the out-door circulation of *bank notes*, are required to maintain the rate of interest normally at three per cent. So long as this relative supply of a circulating medium is maintained, a state of growing national prosperity should always result: the moderate value of money being ever the mainspring, the *prime mover* in our industrial activity.

But, now, let 10 millions of gold be withdrawn from the Bank, for any purpose, and the basis of the superstructure of our industry and commerce is at once undermined and shattered. What was before an enviable state of advancing prosperity is suddenly transformed into a most terrible and universal calamity!

Still, whatever will *replace the ebbing bullion* at the Bank as fast as it is drained away, would, of course, avert the impending calamity from the country, and from the Bank.

Therefore, if nothing else be done during the drain of gold, let there be simply an issue of Bank notes, of such *low denomination* as will enable them to do that work of the circulation, which is now restricted to *gold* and *silver*, in consequence of the lowest denomination of Bank notes being £5.

As a second mode of solution, therefore, let there be issued, in exchange for so much gold and silver taken out of the circulation, Bank notes of such reduced denomination as £2 10s., £2, £1 10s., £1, and even of 10s.; the Bank offering a very small premium on the specie so received in exchange for the small notes, to repay the expense and trouble of the provincial banks in collecting it.

Afterwards, when again the foreign drain had satisfied itself, a very small premium offered by the Bank, for the return of these small notes, would induce the banks at large to re-collect them ; to be again received by the Bank of Issue in exchange for gold and silver to be thus restored to the circulation; and so withdraw again from circulation the small notes.

Our domestic reserves of specie would *alone* thus meet the emergency, and having done so satisfactorily, would be also readily replenished again, to furnish provision against any future similar exigency of a foreign drain.

And why should *this* simple expedient not be resorted to ? Because, as we conceive, such has been the lamentable *misconception* prevalent on this whole subject, that no effective provision for a drain of gold has yet been deemed a *necessity* at all ; but. on the other hand, the Bank's *profit* has been made to *rise* just in proportion as she *neglects* to secure this provision, so indispensable to the public.

An objection may be raised to this plan, based

G

on a prejudice against the *smaller* notes, which prejudice had been fostered by Sir Robert Peel, when he unwisely, as we think, abolished them. Is not a security, which is deemed sufficient for a *Thousand Pound* note, equally good for a note of *Ten shillings* denomination? Who would dispute this?

Such smaller notes would, without doubt, efficiently and acceptably provide for the payment of *industrial wages*, and for the conduct of the great *Retail* trade of the country; while the gold and silver, received by the Bank in exchange for such small notes,—if these latter were issued in the proportion of, say, *two* millions of notes for each *million* of gold *drained* from the Bank for export,—would steadily augment the *proportion* of gold to the aggregate of the Bank notes issued of all denominations; instead of its being *diminished*, as it is now, with every million of gold lost through the drain : in other words, the proportion of *gold* to the total of notes would be expanded. The proposed issue of small notes would augment the *aggregate* of Bank Notes; but it would also augment the Bank's *specie* in a greater *ratio*.

A very simple illustration will shew this to be the case: For, let the Bank, under the existing system, suffer a loss of five millions of gold through a foreign drain; the gold in the Bank previously being 20 millions, and the paper issues 35 millions; each million of gold so lost extinguishing so much paper :—

	Millions. Gold.	Millions. Issues.
Prior to the drain	20	35
Loss by drain	5	5
Proportion of gold, 50 per cent. . . .	15	30
And on a further drain of	5	5
Proportion of gold, 40 per cent. . . .	10	25

Now, compare this result with the effect of a
similar drain, corrected by the proposed issue of
small notes :—

	Gold.	Issues.
Prior to the drain	20	35
Loss by drain	5	5
	15	30
Add gold received for small notes . . .	10	10
Proportion of gold, 62½ per cent. . . .	25	40
And on a further drain of	5	5
	20	35
Add gold received for small notes . . .	10	10
Proportion of gold, 66⅔ per cent. . . .	30	45

Thus it is clear, that while, under the present
system, the proportion of gold to issues diminishes
with every loss of gold: Under the proposed issue
of small notes, it *augments* by each issue of such
notes in exchange for specie. For, while under the
present system, the proportion of gold to issues,
would be reduced to *forty* per cent. : it would, under
the proposed plan be increased to *sixty-six* and
two-thirds per cent.

What, indeed, but the most deplorable infatuation could stay the resort to so simple a remedy as
this? A remedy completely within our own power,
and of most certain efficacy, to effect that object for

which the Bank resorts to the futile, but pernicious, expedient, of raising the rate of interest—namely, to maintain her store of bullion.

Now, in 1866, the drain was not an external or a foreign one,[*] but a domestic one; the gold being drawn from the Bank mainly, we presume, to furnish the increased amount of circulation required in the *provinces*, chiefly for the increased payment of wages, owing to the active condition of our national industry.

Why, then, was not the issue of small notes promptly adopted to meet this merely domestic exigency, and by their taking effectually the place of gold and silver, release such gold and silver from active duty in the circulation, and cause them to return to the Bank, in exchange for each issue of small notes: thus maintaining intact the bullion basis of the Bank.

It is a fact, of course, now well ascertained, that *unemployed* money cannot remain in circulation. It returns to the banks; who also forward their unemployed surplus to the Bank of England. So that each issue of small notes, being in excess of the requirements of money for employment, is an addition to an already full circulation which, so to speak, must cause the latter to overflow; and the surplus so created would return to the banks in gold

[*] Vide Board of Trade Returns: Those for the ten months, ending 31st October, give the Imports, as 30 millions, and the Exports, as only 20 millions sterling.

and silver, these being thus displaced by the issue of small notes.

Now, the domestic circulation of gold and silver is really thus an ample *Domestic Treasury* of our own; from which, temporarily, and without the aid of any *foreign* supply, to draw any required amount, in order thereby to avert the otherwise. disastrous consequences of a drain.

Thus, obviously, and by so simple an expedient, an adequate circulation, and an adequate store of bullion may be permanently maintained: which is the desideratum sought for.

And would there not be perfect freedom from any fear of a *run* being made upon the Bank, by the holders of such small notes,—if these notes were used, as we propose, in such a manner as to become a guarantee and antidote against that failure of *employment* amongst the working classes, which results periodically from the existing money system; and which is the main cause of that public discontent, and those vindictive counsels against our national institutions, which formerly vented themselves in a run upon the Banks?

Let us here remark, that, as is well known to Over-Issues. be the case, a fundamental *fallacy* underlies our whole monetary system : That fallacy is, that there is some *mystic* and recondite relation between *specie* and *paper*; from which, what is denominated *inflation* of prices, must, it is alleged, of necessity result; through what the advocates of this view are pleased to call an *over-issue* of paper.*

With regard to *Over-Issues* of the circulating medium, we may observe that there is perhaps no Currency topic, on which more positive ignorance and absurdity have been displayed than by writers who have undertaken to treat thereof. Under *our* money system an over-issue is simply impossible: because all *excess* in the supply of money is immediately *re-absorbed* by the banks, who again return it to the Bank of England.

The French *Assignats* can afford no *possible* analogy to our Banking system. In the former case, no provision whatever had been made for the re-absorption of an excess in the issues; but the assignats continued to be increasingly issued long after the circulation was full to overflowing; each issue thereafter necessarily serving only to *depreciate* the entire mass of paper.

The same difficulty, in the first instance, presented itself shortly after the commencement of the late American war, when the American paper issues also became so rapidly depreciated. But this effect was promptly and effectually remedied, by means of a plan which enabled the Government to re-absorb any excess of paper. The plan was a very simple one—of offering to any holder of Greenbacks a six per cent. Government stock in exchange for them.

The reader will find this moot point ably discussed by the late Mr. Tooke, in his "History of Prices."

So that the holder of such paper, who found himself otherwise unable to employ his money to equal advantage, was thus ensured of at least six per cent. By this provision the American currency became confined within its required limits; and the variation between its *value* and that of *Gold* became afterwards restricted to the mere variations in the market price of the latter, under supply and demand. Even the anomalous speculation of the New York *Gold Ring* fell, under the power of the Secretary to the Treasury; who, being the principal *holder* of Gold, had only to offer to sell that commodity at thirty per cent. below the point to which the Ring had, by a simple manœuvre, run it up; when the whole that singular conspiracy collapsed, and was permanently extinguished.

Does this alleged *inflation* from *over-issues* then present at all a *practical* view of the matter? To test it, let us suppose a circulation, entirely of *gold*, to be so plentiful as to be supplied at a *three* per cent. rate of interest. A three per cent. rate expands the area for the profitable use of money; employment, income, demand, and temporarily enhanced prices of commodities naturally and inevitably result from this stimulus of cheap capital merely. But, though prices are necessarily thus enhanced, until time has been allowed them to cause the inevitably *increased* production of commodities,—enhanced, too, by an exclusively *gold* circulation,—yet this effect it is not to be called *inflation*, according to such authorities, simply because it is not produced by *paper*.

Let us now, therefore, suppose another case: that gold were entirely withdrawn, and a national currency of *paper only* substituted, but which was legislatively prohibited to be supplied from the Bank of issue at any lower rate than *twenty* per cent. interest. The area for the profitable use of money being now circumscribed and restricted by a twenty per cent. rate,—employment, income, demand, all proportionally fail; and prices consequently become gradually reduced, by failure of demand, to possibly fifty per cent. below their range under a three per cent. gold currency. Is it possible then to say that such *depressed* and low prices in paper money are *inflated?* We trow not. They are, indeed, too much *contracted*, and that simply by *paper* money.

Here, too, we may perceive the manner in which the rate of interest, if left to work freely and uninterruptedly, will regulate the prices of produce and manufactures. A low rate will, in the first instance, necessarily stimulate the industrial employment of capital. With the increased expenditure of wages, which is the next result of such industrial activity, the increased *demand* for all commodities will gradually advance their value, —but only in the first instance. For, only let such advanced prices of commodities be maintained long enough, these prices themselves must stimulate such an augmented production of those very

commodities, as must soon reduce such prices
again to their average or normal level. In this way,
a low rate of interest tends *eventually* to promote,
not high prices, but the *lowest* scale of prices that
is consistant with supply and demand; although such
low value of money seemed, at first, to tend only in
the opposite direction. With a high rate of interest
the results, of course, are all *vice versâ.*

With regard to the interesting question of *Con-* Convertibility.
vertibility in a Bank note circulation,—although ourselves advocates of a convertible currency, we must
here observe that convertibility is, by no means, an
essential in the circulating medium. On this point,
argument would be superfluous : while we are
enabled to appeal to the commercial experience of
America during the last ten years, under such an inconvertible currency. Indeed, we sincerely wish our
more eminent financial authorities would candidly
analyse this American experiment, in all its bearings
and results; and receive therefrom the practical
information and valuable light it is certainly well
calculated to afford an enquirer in this branch of our
subject. Excepting, perhaps, some very trivial
inconveniencies merely, the national, inconvertible
Greenbacks, have obstructed neither productive
industry nor commercial enterprise, nor whether the
latter were foreign or domestic, but have sustained
and advanced every national interest. They have
supplied the sinews to a great war, and they are now

106

accomplishing rapidly the liquidation of the public debt created by that unparalleled contest!

The Essentials in a Currency. What is *essential* in a currency, or circulating medium, is, that it should, first of all, supply a *Measure* applicable to *Value:* just as the yard, of 36 inches, is applied as a measure of *bulk*. The Pound sterling—sub-divided into 20 shillings, or 240 pence,—constitutes this measure of value in this country.

As a measure, merely, neither the yard measure, nor the pound sterling need possess other, or *intrinsic*, value. Without a *medium*-of exchange, and a measure of value, one commodity, of course, might still be exchanged against another, by barter; but the process of such exchanges, and of ascertaining the relative value of one commodity compared with another, must be only a very clumsy and capricious one, and such as could not co-exist with modern civilisation.

But with a reliable *measure* of value, the Farmer, for example, who now desires by the sale of his wheat, to procure other commodities for his establishment,—first fixes a *price* upon his wheat, and so *measures* its *value* to the eye of any purchaser. The farmer in like manner finds the value of the commodities he wishes to procure, also measured by the prices placed upon them; so that he is at no trouble as to ascertaining whether such commodities are equivalents for what he has to offer in exchange for them. The exchange, however, is not a *direct* one, but is made through a money-*medium*, which is both a *measure*, as being a *price* also itself; and, likewise, from its inherent value, a *power* to command the possession of any commodity of equal value. The farmer, having obtained that money for his produce, passes it on again in exchange for the commodities he purchases; and the money-medium, so circulating from hand to hand, when it has thus passed through a thousand hands, has performed payments, or has become the medium of exchange for commodities, which, in the aggregate, are a *thousand times* the value of the sum of *money* received by the farmer, in the first instance, in exchange for his wheat.

From this it will be evident, that, when the circulating medium is arbitrarily contracted, the value of what is so abstracted from the circulation, as so much *money* merely, is of small consideration in itself, compared with the thousand times greater value of the exchanges, of which it has been the medium : and which are now rendered impracticable through its withdrawment.

For, it must be manifest, that every £1000 of the currency, in so passing from hand to hand a thousand times, will have paid an aggregate of £1,000,000! Such indeed is the incalculable importance of even each £1000 of the circulating medium. The mischief, therefore, which must result from the arbitrary withdrawal of only that insignificant amount, from the useful exchanges it was performing throughout the country, is likewise incalculable. What then must be the extent of mischief produced when the withdrawal of the circulating medium is not by thousands, but by *millions* sterling, and must be felt in every corner and by every trader in the land?

Thus it is too, that the money-*medium* of exchange,—into which medium all commodities must now be converted before such commodities can be exchanged—supersedes, in the most perfect manner, the primitive mode of exchange, by direct barter of one commodity against another.

It will be evident from this account, that, since every commodity and production can only now be exchanged by being first passed through this money-medium; the money-medium itself,—like a Bridge which has to convey the traffic from each side of it,—must be large enough to admit of every commodity being converted into it, requiring to be exchanged : Otherwise, just in the same manner as the traffic over a too contracted and ill-adapted bridge, is necessarily thrown into confusion and arrested ; so, if any sudden and arbitrary contraction shall befall the circulating medium in the midst of the exchanges it is beneficially effecting, the exchange of commodities must be contracted or arrested, to the confusion and injury of the producers and traffickers. The contraction or stoppage of the traffic on our main lines of *railway*, for a few weeks, would equally serve to illustrate the ill effects of an arbitrary contraction of the circulation.

It is, therefore, above all things, *essential* in a currency, that, whatever be its composition, it should at all times be maintained in ample relative supply to the duty it has to perform, since it is the only medium in which the exchanges of the industrial productions of the country through which it circulates, can be effected; and any failure in that respect, only places the country depending upon it, in a condition infinitely worse than could have resulted from even the more primitive mode of exchange by barter.

In the next place, as a *medium of exchange*, a recognised *interest value* is an *essential* element in the circulating medium. In semi-barbarous and primitive times, when credit money was unknown, —gold and silver alone afforded this requisite exchangeable value. But, in our more civilised times, we know that one of the most valuable of properties is a national *Funded Debt*, of *eight hundred millions* sterling; possessing a recognised interest and exchangeable value, although represented by nothing whatever of *intrinsic* value : its whole value to the holder, being simply the national *promise* to pay £3 per annum on each £100 of the debt! It is this *three per cent. return* on the investment of £100, which constitutes the relative value of this stock compared with that of other property; it is the *promise* by the *Government* to pay the interest,

which constitutes the *inherent* and sole security of
the stock : And, we may ask, what property has a
more real or marketable value, than three per cent.
Consols ?

If *gold* be essential to give value to a currency,
what then, we demand, gives value to our *irredeemable* Funded Debt, of £800,000,000? Could not
the same National security give equal value to a
National *Currency*, though also irredeemable?
The National Debt has been saleable at nearly
its par value, and has actually commanded the *par*
of 100 sovereigns, for £100 of the stock : Could not
a National currency, if also issued at three per cent.,
be in the same manner maintained at or near the
par of 100 sovereigns for £100 of the National
currency? With this decisive fact before us, further
argument is indeed superfluous.

Either of the two suggested plans of reform
would, doubtless, supply the desideratum sought for.
We have presumed to submit no personal *hobby*, or
mere *crotchet* of our own. Any *other* arrangement
which would equally afford security to the country,
that the Bullion in the Bank *shall be maintained* up
to such a level as will adequately *sustain the great
interests based upon it*, would be *equally* satisfactory
to ourselves.

In pursuing this discussion, we have endeavoured
to relieve it from the prejudice and mystery with
which the subject is ordinarily invested : content to
treat it *practically*, as a very simple question : which

indeed it is ; and so to rest our argument only on undisputed, historical and extant *facts :* and these, to every unbiassed mind, should be conclusive. And, with regard to *one* suggested practical *solution* of the important question with which we have dealt, we cannot doubt that any Commercial House, accustomed to similar transactions, would only be too glad to undertake the required duty of furnishing the matter-of-fact *remedy* required, for the remuneration of a commission of one per cent.; the Government bearing the cost of transport, and issuing the necessary amount of Consols, as a basis for the operation.

The circulating medium of a country is the National *Highway of Commerce.* It must, therefore, be of the very first importance, that the Legislature should give precedence to this requirement, over, perhaps, every other State question : should provide, and maintain, in a condition of the greatest efficiency, this prime national desideratum. Its direct bearing upon the moral, civil and material interests of the State, as well as of each member of the body politic, is such, indeed, as to constitute it the main *basis* of all that is vital to a nation's prosperity.

To neglect this indispensable provision, is to place the country very much in the same situation as an Estate in an American prairie,—rich in mineral wealth and productive soils,—but debarred from every market, by the *want of roads* of communication.

Doubtless, therefore, were a National currency to be so constituted, that it should never be issued at any lower rate than *three* per cent; and should never be able, while in circulation, to fall *below* three per cent., such a currency would possess, of course, precisely the *same* security as Consols, for its being maintained at three per cent.; and the same security as Consols also for its inherent value to the holder. By means, possibly, of some plan similar to that adopted by the American Government, when they offered in exchange a six per cent. stock to any holder of surplus currency; our Government might be authorised to issue three per cent. Consols in exchange for any surplus notes : or, the same object might be effected by the *sale* of securities.

Now, just as any interest-bearing property would be valued according as it returned either five, or ten per cent. : So, a currency, assured of being maintained at three per cent., must have a relative value, compared with such property, in the ratio which three per cent. bears, either to the five or to ten per cent. return derived from such other property.

Such a National currency, therefore, must possess the essential attributes,—of being, first, a *Measure* of *Value;* and, next, of being, a *Standard* of *Value* to all other property: which are the desiderata required.

As a National currency, like that described, would be equally as *exchangeable* as Consols: So it

would possess the needful purchasing power with
regard to all other commodities ; including, of
course, gold and silver : which latter commercial
commodities would vary in value, as other commodities do, according to their relative supply in
market ; but the inherent and interest value of the
currency, would, at all times, remain invariably the
same.

For *domestic* purposes, it is obvious from this
representation, that such a currency could always be
issued in adequate supply, independently of gold.
In *international* commerce, the relative price of gold
would be taken into the calculation ; but without
either difficulty or delay to transactions : precisely
as international trade is now regularly, and with
facility, carried on between America and the rest of
the commercial world.

On such considerations then, we submit, that
convertibility, although to be preferred, is not an
essential condition in the circulating medium ; since,
when deprived of that attribute, it can then perform, as in America, all the functions of a currency,
both for State and commercial objects which a gold
currency could accomplish, and indeed, in some
respects, more efficiently.

How then can such paper issues *necessarily* produce inflation! Is it not a question simply of the
rate of *interest*, at which the circulating medium, be
it what it may, is to be obtained?

It is to us thus self-evident, that it is the rate of

interest only, and not convertibility that can maintain
—were such a result to be desired,—a high value in
the circulating medium, in relation to the value of all
other commodities: which the rate of interest must
absolutely govern and control.

An investment, for example, in any property
paying *ten* per cent., is *ceteris paribus* intrinsically
worth *double* the price we should pay for the same
property if it returned only *five* per cent. per annum.
So with every form of investment whatever; as well
as with the money itself; and thus it should, we
think, be self-evident, that this fancied mystic property of *gold*, compared with paper, is simply a
dangerous illusion: It is the *rate* at which money
can be obtained, and nothing else, which must
regulate its purchasing power, over those commodities for which it has to be exchanged.

Any property, whatever, calculated, on the
average of years, to return *ten* per cent. per annum,
must be worth just double of what it would be
worth, if it returned only *five* per cent. ; and in the
same way precisely, money, or the currency, which
on an average of years was ascertained to yield ten
per cent. interest, would have double the purchasing
power it would possess, if its interest value, on an
average of years, were ascertained to be only five
per cent.

Such a national currency as that just referred
to, is, of course, one which it is in the power and
within the province of the Legislature to *create:*

although to create a *gold* one, is not so. Such a
currency too can, by the Legislature, be maintained
in just such supply as that it could neither fall *below*,
nor rise *above* three per cent. ; and it is not possible
that such a three per cent. currency,—although it
would necessarily establish a condition of national
prosperity, and, in consequence, augment the demand
for, and the price of commodities,—would more do so
than a purely *gold* currency would, if issued also at
three per cent. ; nor could it, more than the latter
would, *inflate* prices in any different or greater
degree than must be always incident to any currency
of like moderate interest value. For the area within
which capital finds profitable employment must
expand in exact ratio as the rate of interest *declines*,
and *vice versa*. And from these considerations, it
seems to us to result, that the circulating medium of
a great country like ours, is a thing so purely
artificial, that it is certainly competent to the Legislature to introduce a perfectly effective currency, as
we see in America to-day ; or a thoroughly and
viciously defective one, just like our own.

And here we must be allowed to observe, that
such a National currency, whatever defects may be
imputed to it, would at least be an *honest* one : Its
notes would not bear, on their face, like those of the
Bank of England, the illusory *promise* and preposterous *pretence*, of being payable in gold on demand :
but still the national notes would enable the holder,
who desired their conversion into gold for foreign

commercial transactions, to purchase that commodity at the market price, even with such, so called, " inconvertible " paper !

The country has, generally, been induced to sympathise with the Bank, whenever it has been threatened with insolvency—that is to say, with inability to pay its notes in gold,—just as though the Nation itself were involved in such discredit. But it certainly is not so. If the Bank makes a promise on the face of its notes, with only 10s. in hand, to pay 20s. in the pound, and at the same time neglects, as no other mercantile concern dare do, to provide the needful means for redeeming such promise ; the discredit belongs exclusively to the Bank, and she alone should pay the penalty. But when a National Currency is issued —which neither makes nor requires any such promise, as we see exemplified in the current American Greenbacks,—any discredit of that kind becomes, of course, an impossibility. The circulating medium, so issued, must maintain its relative value, just as £100 of our 3 per cent. *irredeemable* Consols would, were that £100 to be subdivided into 100 equal parts, and sent into the country as authorised legal tender.

A Working Man's Question.

Finally—we must now submit that this is emphatically a *Working Man's* question, and one of the most vital importance to his class. The well-being of our Artizans is necessarily in exact proportion to the abundance and steadiness of *employment*, at full and remunerative wages; which again depends upon the activity of trade and *remunerative markets* for the productions of our various branches of industry. This is national prosperity. And the working man's position is good or bad, as this condition of things, or its reverse, may alternately obtain.

Now, with the return of a condition of prosperity,—the attendant rise of prices, the expansion of employment, and the advance of the rate of wages, necessitate a proportionate expansion of the *circulation*; for if the previous supply of money had only been adequate to the demands of a more restricted employment, an increase of the latter, say, by *ten per cent.*, could not be met except by a similar augmentation of the monetary means required for the increased amount of payments.

But, for the payment of *wages*, our lowest denomination of Bank notes,—£5, is useless; and the needful amount of *specie* must take its place in that branch, as well as over the entire area of the immense *Retail* trade of the country.* Let us, therefore, assume that the general estimate of some 100 millions of gold and silver is correct enough, as

---

* It may well be surmised, that the Government was unable to appreciate the importance of an adequate supply of *silver*, for the payment of wages at all points, proportioned to the increased amount of employment, at the advanced rate of wages, consequent upon our recent prosperity; or the Chancellor of the Exchequer could not have turned a deaf ear to the appeals, repeatedly made to him, to issue an additional amount of silver coinage to meet the exigency. It is indeed not easy to over-estimate the inconvenience, and positive hardship and suffering, to which a large portion of the population may be subjected from this simple cause—the want of such a small denomination of money as will serve for the payment of *wages*.

to the amount of specie so employed in the *normal* state of things: and that the growth of prosperity required, and had absorbed from the Bank, 10 per cent increase, or *ten millions* sterling. Now, if, unfortunately the Bank's reserve, by this process, should have been reduced by an equal amount, an inevitable money crisis must, of course, be the result.

Thus it is, that a state of great prosperity, in which the working population are fully and steadily employed, is a thing utterly *impossible*, under our present money system, to be permanently maintained: for, sooner or later, this condition of prosperity, how essential soever it may be to the well-being of the working classes,—by its simple action upon the Bank, as described, must work its own overthrow. This is the consequence of that *failure of demand* for industrial productions in the market,—the design and the result, as we have seen from the evidence of our highest financial authorities, of the Bank's procedure. The effect is, in the very highest condition of prosperity attainable, by means of a rude contraction of the needful money facilities, to *close our markets;* and, with them, to *close* or place on *short time* our great *manufactories* and other concerns; and, at the same time, to *turn adrift the working man*, through the length and breadth of the land: until the *gold*, now no longer capable of active and profitable employment, in consequence of this universal depreciation of commodities, returns again in *millions* to the Bank. The abettors of this ruthless policy must needs now claim a triumph, in virtue solely of these terribly "successful" results!

We are told that Nero fiddled while Rome was burning. But in our humble opinion, it were better for our country and more creditable to ourselves, that such indecorous exultations over miseries caused to others by ourselves, were altogether restricted to an *age*, and a *character* like those of the Imperial miscreant just named.

We cannot envy its advocates this distinguished success of their policy. *Such* success appears to us its most decisive condemnation. We are here, indeed, reminded of a pertinent and beautiful story in one of Addison's Spectators: In which a certain Sultan, who, by needless wars, had depopulated his country,—walking out one day with his Vizier, who, whether as a humourist or an enthusiast, professed to understand the language of *Birds:* when the Sultan, espying two Owls perched upon some neighbouring ruins, desired the Vizier to listen, and report the subject of their conversation. Returning, he thus addressed the Monarch: "Sire, you must know, that these two owls have been negotiating a contract of marriage, between the son of the one and the daughter of the other: in which it has been agreed, that each parent shall settle upon his offspring a *hundred ruined Villages:* the parent owls chanting in chorus, — "Long live Sultan

Mahmoud, that we may never want ruined villages to settle upon our children!"

The direst foe of mankind, we think, may well take up this strain, and sing: " Long live the Bank Charter Act,"—that nationally oppressive and ruinous rates of Interest may never fail to reward their distinguished Advocates, while useless millions of gold lie unemployed in Bank; that countless myriads of discharged Artisans may never be wanting to recruit the ranks of unemployed, pauperised, and disaffected Working Men, with their starving wives and families ; that Usury may flourish, and our many Industries lie prostrate and languish under the fearful, but inevitable visitation, *at least once in every decade,* of a withering, desolating, and universal MONEY PANIC!

APPENDIX.—I.

—••—

Week ending Aug.	21, 1872	..			£123,610,000
"	"	"	28,	"	94,359,000
"	"	Sept.	4,	"	124,328,000
"	"	"	11,	"	94,979,000
"	"	"	18,	"	118,792,000
"	"	"	25,	"	94,004,000
"	"	Oct.	2,	"	124,085,000
"	"	"	9,	"	111,615,000
"	"	"	16,	"	125,766,000
"	"	"	23,	"	108,835,000
"	"	"	30,	"	117,164,000
"	"	Nov.	6,	"	107,273,000
"	"	"	13,	"	93,780,000

In 13 Weeks......£1,438,590,000

Which sum, multiplied by 4 for the whole year,
would give 5,754,360,000

To which must be added (an unknown sum) for
Bills retired elsewhere ; the Manchester Clear-
ing-house alone retiring 60 to 70 millions
sterling per annum ; the aggregate, say, is 50
per cent. of the above amount ; or...... 2,877,180,000

There must be further added the gross amount of
all the *Cash* payments subject to discount,—
not less, probably, than three-fourths of the
aggregate of both of the above items; or ... 6,473,655,000

Thus we have, for the year's payments, an area
covered by each advanced rate of interest, of...£15,105,195,000

The first item is, of course, official, and undisputed ; and of itself sustains
the argument. The remaining figures are necessarily guesses merely,
although proximate.

If the average term of the Bills, &c., were *four* months, each advance
of interest would apply to over *one-third* of the above gross aggregate. This
item we have deduced, for illustration, in round figures, as being 5,000
millions sterling.

But *one-fourth* only of this amount would, of course, more than suffice for
our argument.

EFFICACY of the French plan of remedying a Drain of Specie, namely, by simply declaring *Bank Notes* to be *legal tender :* as depicted in the following extract from the *Times*, of the 16th February, 1849 :—

"As a mere commercial speculation, with the assets which the Bank held in its hands, it might then have stopped payment, and liquidated its affairs with every probability that a very few weeks would enable it to clear off all its liabilities. But this idea was not for a moment entertained by M. D'Argout, and he resolved to make every effort to keep alive what may be termed the *circulation of the life blood* of the community. The task was overwhelming. Money was to be found to meet not only the demands on the Bank, but the necessities, both public and private, of every rank in society. It was essential to enable the Manufacturers to work, lest their workmen, driven to desperation, should fling themselves amongst the most violent enemies of public order. It was essential to provide money for the food of Paris, for the pay of the troops, and for the daily support of the *ateliers nationaux*. A failure on any one point would have led to a fresh convulsion. But the panic had been followed by so great a scarcity of the metallic currency, that a few days later, out of a payment of 26 millions fallen due, only 47,000 francs could be recovered in silver.

" In this extremity, when the Bank alone retained any available sums of money, the Government came to the rescue, and, on the night of the 15th of March, the *notes of the Bank* were by a decree made a *legal tender*, the issue of these notes being limited in all to 350 millions, but the amount of the lowest of them reduced for the public convenience to 100 francs. One of the great difficulties mentioned in the report, was to print these 100 franc notes fast enough for the public consumption,—in ten days the amount issued in this form had reached 80 millions. No sooner was the Bank relieved from the necessity of paying away the remnant of its coin, than it made every exertion to increase its metallic rest. About 40 millions of silver were purchased abroad at a high price. More than 100 millions were made over in dollars to the Treasury and the executive departments in Paris. In all, taking into account the branch Banks, 506 millions of five-franc pieces have been thrown by the Bank into the country since March, and her currency was thus supplied to all the channels of the social system.

" Besides the strictly monetary operations, the Bank of France found means to furnish a series of loans to the Government,—50 millions on exchequer bills on the 31st of March, 30 millions on the 5th of May, and on the 3rd of June 150 millions, to be paid up before the end of March, 1849 ; of this last sum only one-third has yet been required by the State. The Bank also took a part in the renewed loan of 250 millions, and made vast advances to the City of Paris, to Marseilles, to the department of the Seine, and to the hospitals, amounting in all to 260 millions more. But even this was not all. To enable the *Manufacturing* interests to weather the storm, at a moment when all the sales were interrupted, a decree of the National Assembly had directed warehouses to be opened for the reception of all kinds of goods, and provided that the registered invoice of these goods, so deposited, should be made negotiable by endorsement. The Bank of France discounted these receipts. In Havre alone, 18 millions were thus advanced on *Colonial produce*, and, in Paris, 14 millions on *merchandise*,—in all, 60 millions were thus made available for the purposes of trade. Thus, the great institution had placed itself, as it were, in direct contact with every interest of the community, from the Minister of the Treasury down to the trader in a distant outport. Like a huge hydraulic machine, it employed its colossal powers to pump a fresh stream into the exhausted arteries of trade, to sustain credit, and *preserve the circulation from complete collapse.*"

Such were the happy results of this French experiment— of making *Bank Notes a legal tender*—as the simple remedy for a drain of specie.

Let us for a moment suppose that, instead of this beneficent expedient, Lord Overstone's cruel Law of "Contraction" under our Bank Charter Act, had been applied by the French Government as a remedy. No circulating medium, no sales of industrial productions, no employment, no income —must have been the sad result; but, in their place, ghastly want, desperation, and, most certainly, fearful carnage at every point! Except for the timely suspension of the Act during our own Money Crises, the climax of national misery and despair must inevitably ensure amongst ourselves a similar deplorable issue.

And yet, stultified by misleading *Authorities*, and, as if blinded to our destruction, our Legislature only looks on with culpable indifference : trusting *in vain*—as patent facts but too plainly indicate—to futile reductions of some trivial taxes, or to such grand but unavailing panaceas as Free Trade, as antidotes to the still rapid and *defiant* growth amongst us, of destitution, pauperism, and crime ! Would, indeed, that a patriotic Government,—discarding hereafter all *theory* which has only a *name* to recommend it, and recognising the *Public Good* alone as the object of their financial policy,—might rely implicitly on *Experience ;* and, emboldened merely by this simple decisive French *precedent*, as being both *practical* and *satisfactory*, proceed at once, in any future drain of gold, to adopt and sanction an effective *substitute :* thus beneficently *upholding*, instead of barbarously contracting, the National Industry and Commerce depending thereupon ; and, at the same time, averting from us the worst national miseries incident to a Money-panic.

FINIS.

www.ingramcontent.com/pod-product-compliance
Lightning Source LLC
Chambersburg PA
CBHW030619270326
41927CB00007B/1240